Marcello Palace

INSTANT PIANO

Play piano without having to read the notes

The classic piano repertoire in Keyboard Language Multiline (MT)

A unique and revolutionary system of reading and writing keyboard music graphically, without having to read notes

~Self-teaching version~

Learn in a week what it takes months to learn with conventional music notation:

no ear playing,

no outstanding memory needed,

Just for everybody..!

INSTANT PIANO

Spend more time playing the piano and less time learning to play.

If playing piano is such a joyful thing, why do we need to study so much theory even to play the simplest piece of music?

The KeyLang Multiline MT system is the alternative to the tiring and time-consuming process needed to learn to play piano music with the traditional music notation. With KeyLang Multiline MT you avoid learning the complex musical system that was created centuries ago. With an approach from the 21st century, you just sit down and play piano music, from the first moment and without further delays.

After my university studies, I have been teaching piano for years. In all this time as a teacher, I have seen many people frustrated and giving up their dream of playing the piano just because of the complicated learning process that the traditional method implies. The truth is that before playing a simple tune, with the traditional music method it is necessary to learn sophisticated concepts of key signatures and music theory. Precisely because of that, many students are put off because the equation "time investment / results" is not adding up. Although in some cases the traditional method of learning of music is still advisable, it has become clear that something different and more tuned to the modern lifestyle is necessary, especially for those who just want to learn to enjoy music as a hobby and valuable pastime. Furthermore, even professional musicians frequently wish to dedicate more time to the practical creation of music rather than learning the tedious theory behind the traditional notation.
In this book I present a modern music system that does not need translation from what you see on the paper to the keyboard. The KeyLang Multiline MT system reduces to a minimum the learning of the music language, you play what you see. This characteristic of my method represents a huge advantage from the traditional system, where you spend 80% of the time learning to read music and only 20% actually playing piano. Although with KeyLang Multiline MT system you still need to spend some time mastering the musical pieces, rest assured that you will be most of the time learning piano and not theory. What is more…you will be listening to the music coming out of your hands as soon as you sit on the piano!

KeyLang Multiline is for everybody, adults and children. No matter the availability of practice time you have, you will always be able to play the piano in a flash. Additionally, you can always undertake the study of traditional music notation because the structure of the symbols used by the Multiline system does not contradict the traditional notation system from which has borrowed elements as well. KeyLang Multiline MT system is the modern answer to your musical needs!

The Creator of the KeyLang Multiline MT System
Marcello Palace

HOW TO READ MUSIC WRITTEN IN MULTILINE KEYBOARD LANGUAGE

When it comes to learning to read a conventional music sheet, you need to go through a long training process so that it will take months before you get to play a reasonable piece of music. With the KeyLang system you skip that process so we invest 100% of the time playing the piano instead. Thus, whilst for conventional music you need training in theory and learning to read the notes prior sitting at the piano/keyboard, with the KeyLang Multiline [MT] system we reduce the tedious study of music theory to just *indications* that take minutes to learn. In order to be consistent with our promise let's start a quick look to those basic indications needed to play the piano or keyboard.

SPEED OF MUSIC

Before we start playing music we determine a pulse. Every music piece have a pulse and having that pulse clear in our mind will help us to give every note the correct duration. If we don't respect the duration of the notes the music can become as unrecognisable as when you take away punctuation from a paragraph in a book.

The musical pulse can go as slow as 40 beats a minute as well as over 200 beats a minute. If the speed of a musical piece (called *tempo*) is for example 60, we have one beat per second. Look at your watch and try tapping on the table at the rate of one beat per second; that will give you the idea.
It's common for everyone to start tapping our feet at the sound of music. It is quite common for musicians to do that as they play too.

Musicians use a tool called *METRONOME* to determine and follow a pulse with precision. If you search for "online metronome" on the Internet you'll find dozens of online metronomes that will help you to play and determine the different tempos.

RIGHT HAND – LEFT HAND

In order to quick identify notes that belong to each hand we set the round or oval notes as the ones to be played by the right hand and the square or rectangular as the ones to be played by the left hand.

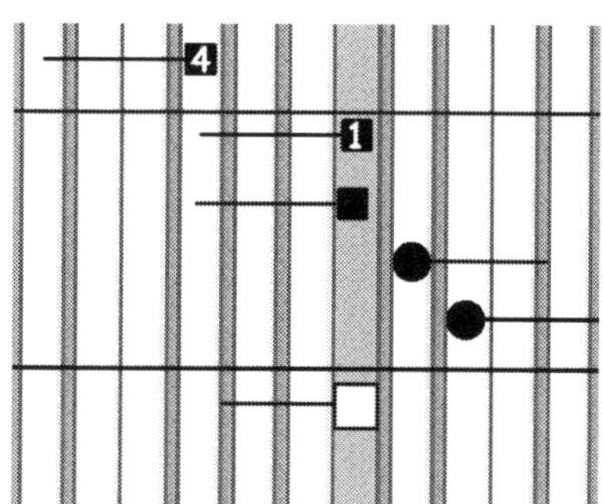

In addition, if a note has stems (those horizontal tails), the right hand notes stems will usually point to the right and the left hand ones stems to the left

DIRECTION OF THE READING

When we read music written in KeyLang Multiline system we go from the top down, as we were looking up a name in the white pages. To avoid the order becoming confusing or when a note or set of notes is played simultaneously with another note which several keys away from each other, we use dotted lines like these ones:

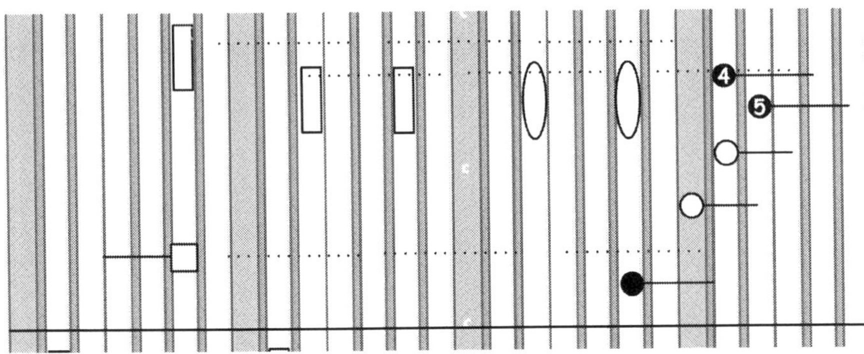

FINGER NUMBERS

You'll notice numbers inside some of the notes. These are finger suggestions and indicates which finger we advice you to play that note with:

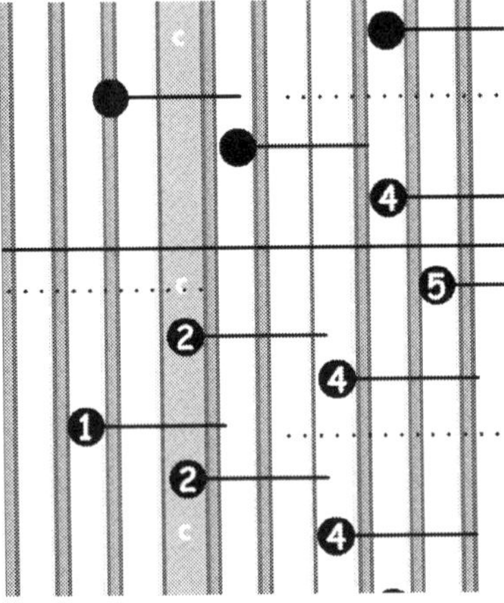

These are the number and the fingers they refer to:
1: Thumb
2: Pointer finger
3: Tall or middle finger
4: Ring finger
5: Little finger or Pinky

This applies likewise on the right or left hand.

LINES AND PIANO KEYS

To be able to know what key to play, we can take as a reference the black keys. If you look closely at a keyboard you'll see blacks keys grouped in an alternating way: Two blacks together, three blacks together, two blacks, three blacks, and so on. If you now look at a music sheet written in KeyLang you'll also find the blacks and white keys depicting the disposition of a real piano or keyboard. So when we see a note placed on that key on a paper we just need to play the same equivalent note in the keyboard. This is the magic of the KeyLang system; you don't need to translate anything.

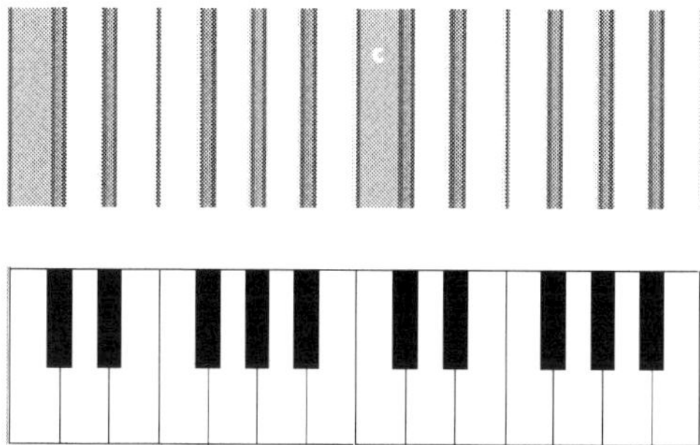

In addition to that, we shaded all the C notes (the white keys on the left of every pair of blacks keys together).

You may place a sticker in some of the C notes on your keyboard at the beginning. That will help you to find the notes easily but you might get used to it too. Avoid it if you want to feel comfortable when playing on someone else's piano.

The middle C on the KeyLang sheets are marked with a white C

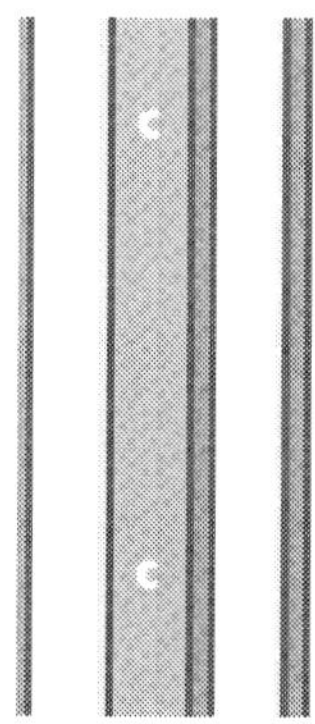

That is for you to identify the middle C. In a piano is usually the closest C to the maker's name.

That's it at the moment let's start playing the piano right away to keep the promise of an instant piano.

HOW TO PLAY "ODE TO JOY"

In our first journey we'll play one of the most famous melodies ever: an extract from Beethoven's 9th Symphony, the Ode to Joy.
We will set our pulse to 108 -search for online metronomes in the Internet to find the tempo- although we can increase the speed as you feel more confident. For every beat we will play a note and a note will look like this for the right hand:

or like this for the left hand:

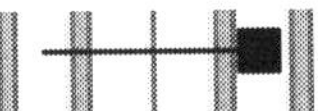

If a note has this aspect (a tail and is black filled inside) we will call this figure a *Quarter*. Different figures have different duration. At the beginning and very often we'll have that a Quarter lasts for a beat. The duration of a bit will depend on the speed we have set to play the piece.

Remember that a number inside some of the notes indicates the finger to use. You don't need to follow it if you don't want to, but if you do, your hands will move smoothly on the keyboard.

We included different versions of this Ode to Joy. It will sound more attractive as we reach to the lasts versions.

ODE TO JOY VERSION 1

On the first version of Ode to Joy we only play Quarters, therefore we will play one note per beat. It's the right hand the one that does all the work (round notes) except for the two notes played by the left hand (square notes). So, set your speed to a pulse of 108 and start playing the notes from the top down, one note per beat. When the page is finished move the page on the right and stop when you find a double horizontal line like this:

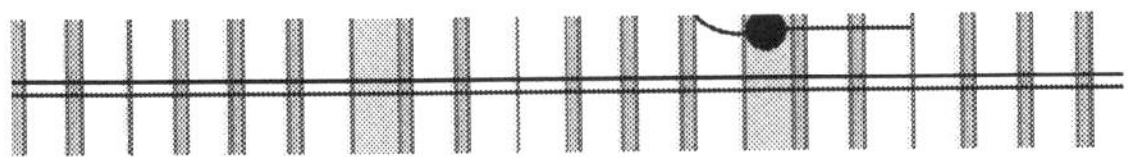

The single horizontal lines like the one we show below, group the notes and make it easy to visualize checkpoints and sometimes to mark musical phrases.

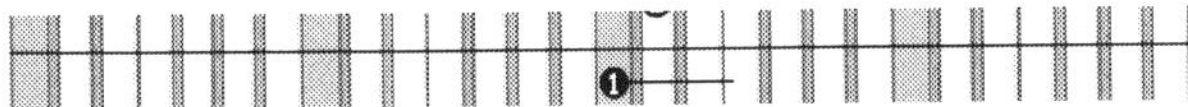

ODE TO JOY VERSION 2

On the second version of the Ode to Joy we merge together some of the Quarters notes with curvy lines that connect two or more notes.

We call them *ties*. Take it as a sort of addition sign. When you see them, play the first Quarter and keep that key pressed for the duration of two beats. Don't lift it to play the second Quarter again. That results in a note that lasts two beats instead of the usual *one-note-per-beat* that we knew so far. You'll notice that the melody now is much more similar to the one that you must be familiar with.

ODE TO JOY VERSION 3

This third version should sound exactly like the Version 2 and the difference is just graphical: we've replaced the two tied Quarter by a round or square white circles that we call Half notes. A Half note will therefore last two beats:

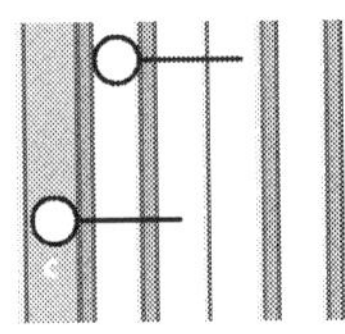

ODE TO JOY VERSION 4

The Version 4 of our Ode to Joy we introduce an Eighth note:

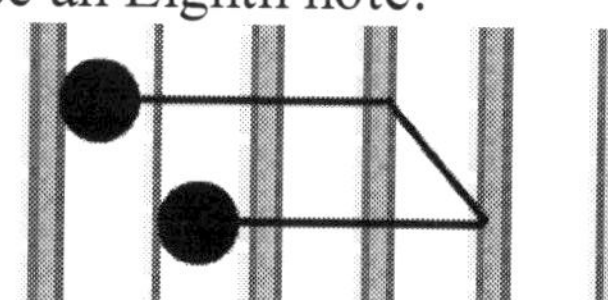

When you see a pair of Eighth notes you have to fit them in one beat, therefore the duration of an Eighth note is exactly half of the duration of an Quarter note.

These notes appear sometimes individually:

We will learn later on this book how to use it.
At the moment let's just play our Ode to Joy Version 4 with the new addition. Now the melody will be even more similar to the one you might be familiar with.

ODE TO JOY VERSION 5

In Version 5 we introduce an active use of the left hand. Squared and rectangular notes are to be played by the left hand. Use the dotted lines to coordinate the two hands, as they will be playing simultaneously this time.
We are also adding a new figure, which we will call the *Whole* note. For the left hand, the Whole note is represented by a standing up rectangle. A right hand Whole by an oval:

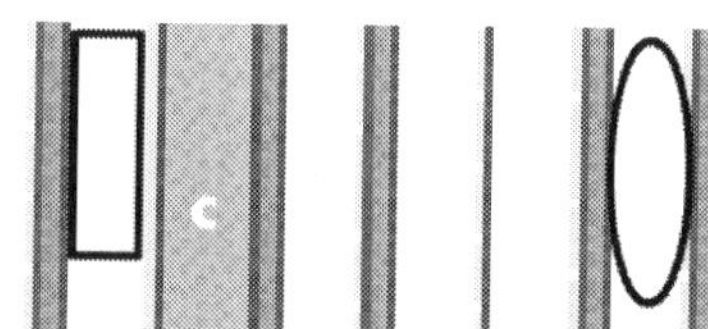

When you see a Whole note you have to keep it ringing for the space of four beats. Many times we will have to run and play another note before we can comply with the four beats duration of the Whole note. In that case you might want to use the right pedal of the piano -sometimes the only pedal available, sometimes not available at all. By pressing the pedal we assure that the Whole notes stay ringing even when you don't finger press them anymore. In this way, you can go using those fingers to play something else in another location of the keyboard. Try not to abuse the use of the pedal if you want to avoid a mushy sound. Lift it every two to four beats approximately.

In our Version 5 and 6 of the Ode to Joy you don't necessary have to use the pedal, as the left hand will be able to keep the notes ringing as indicated.
Try now playing the Version 5.

ODE TO JOY VERSION 6

In our Version 6 we simple add more notes to the left hand to make the music sound more plentiful. Because on the left hand we are using two fingers at the time, it is advisable to be wise in the way we choose the fingers to play it. When no finger is indicated use the finger *5* and *1* to make sure you reach both notes comfortably.
You might need now to work a bit harder in this version, in order to make it sound fluently. The more you play it the more confident you'll get. At the same time you will be exercising your skill to play the oncoming pieces.

Ode to Joy - Version 1

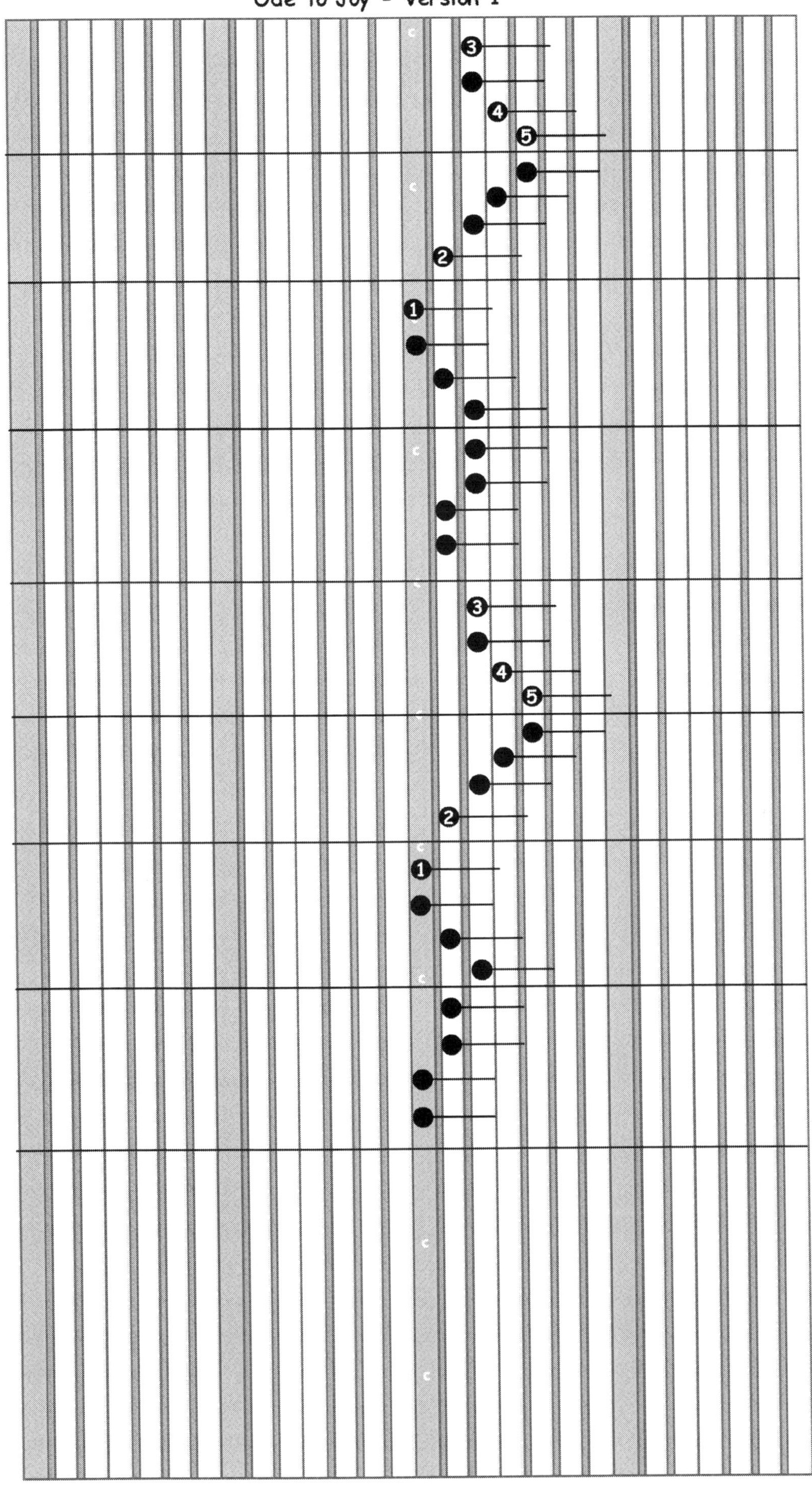

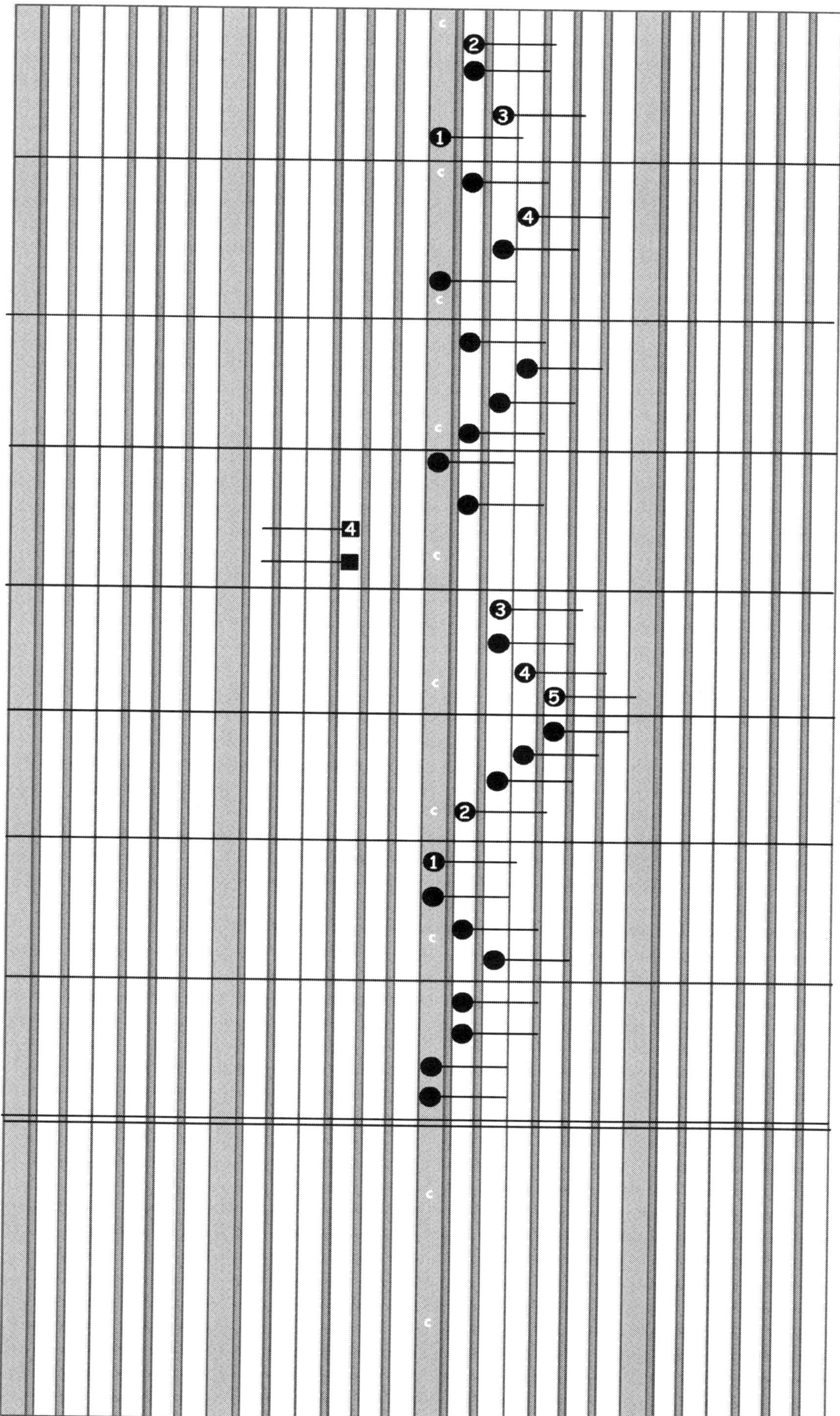

Ode to Joy - Version 2

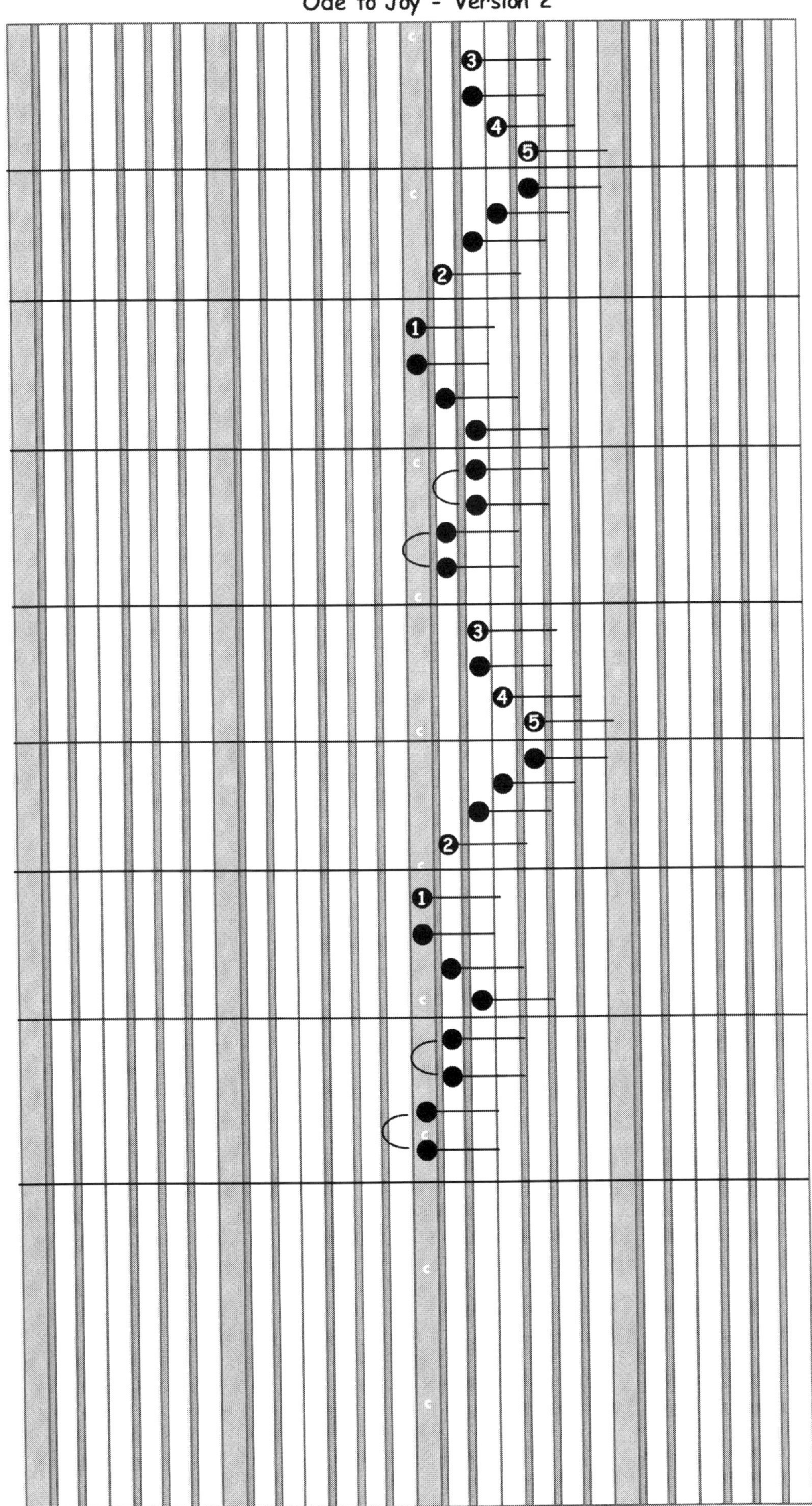

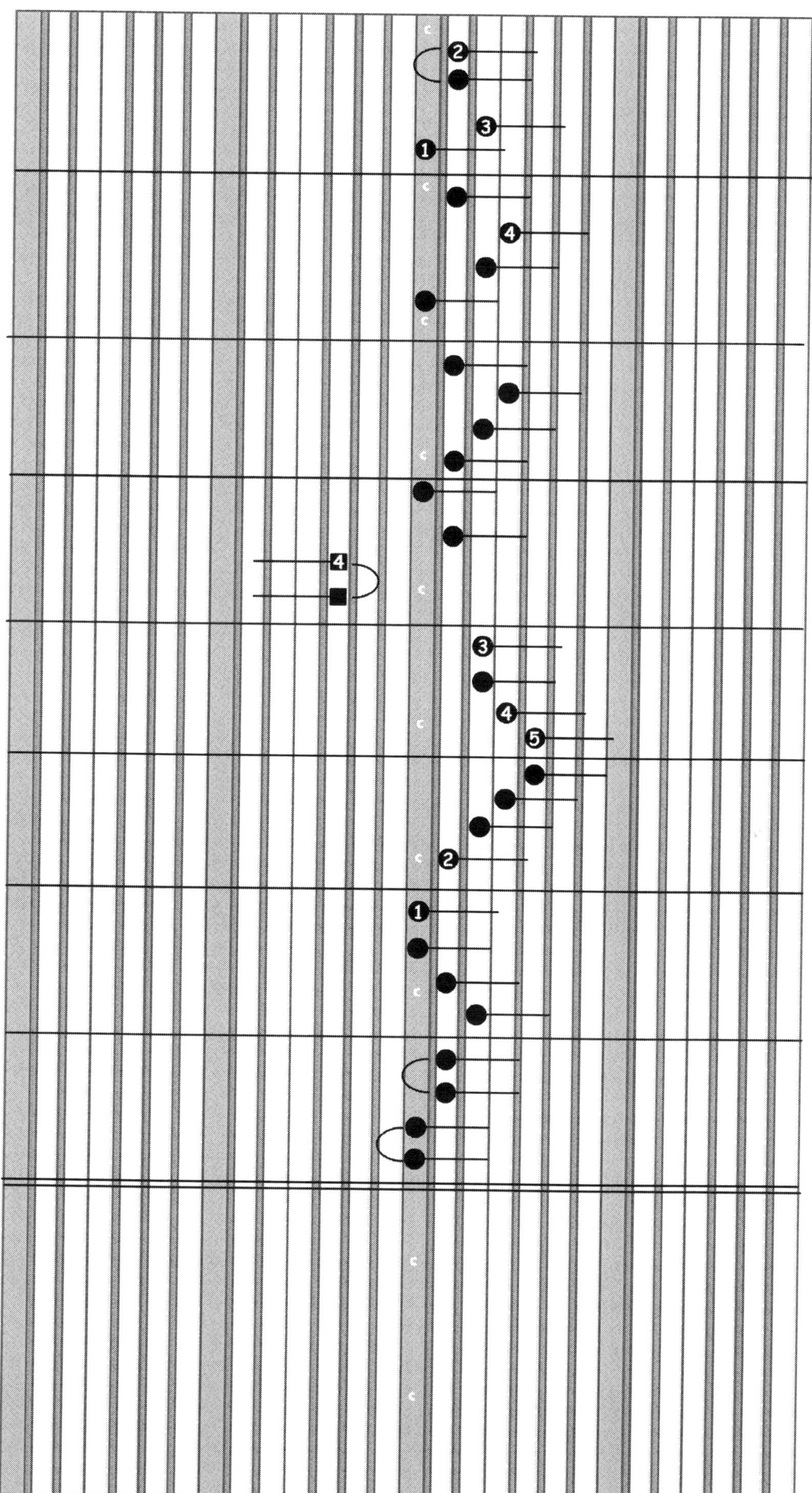

Ode to Joy - Version 3

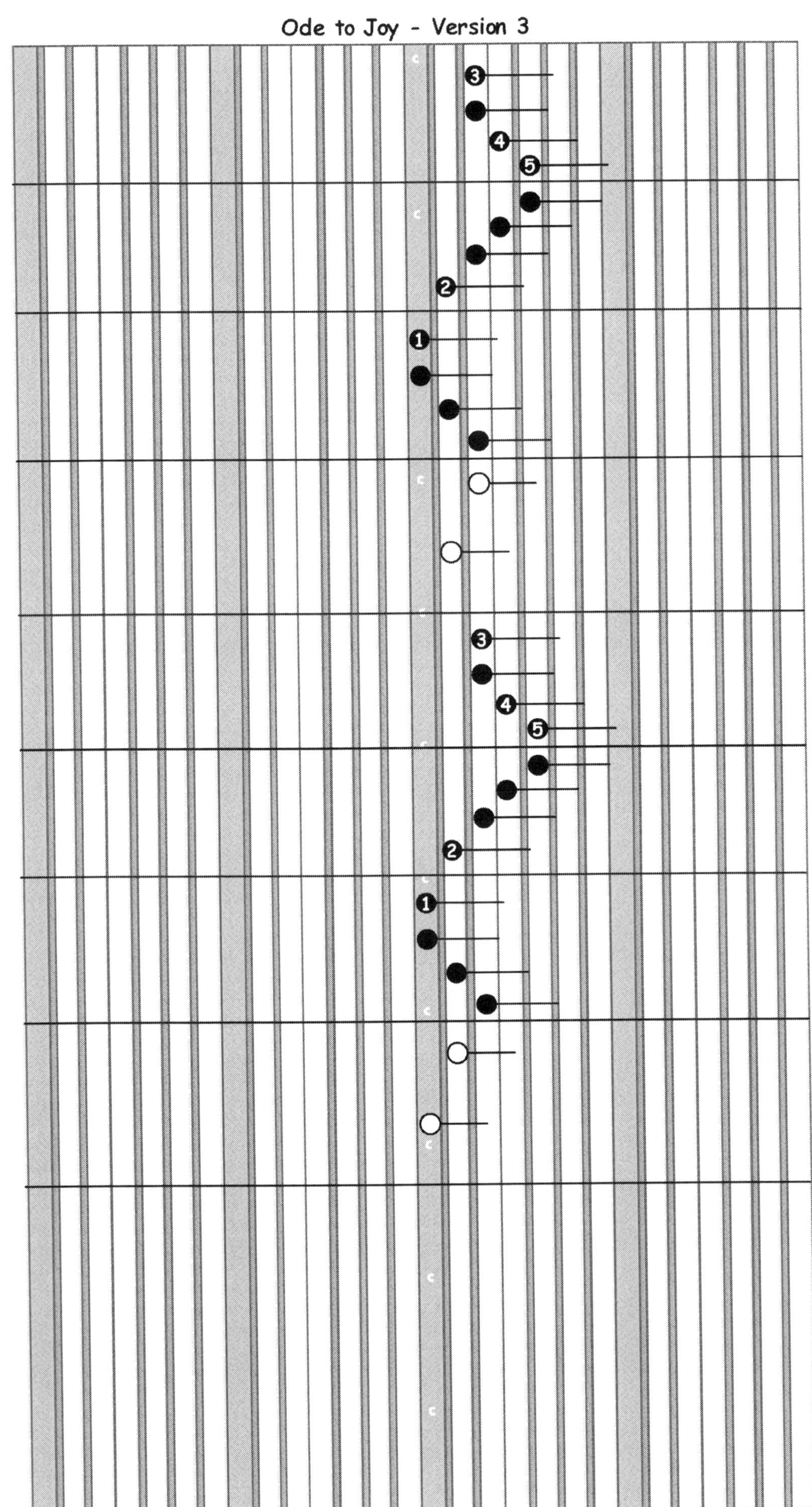

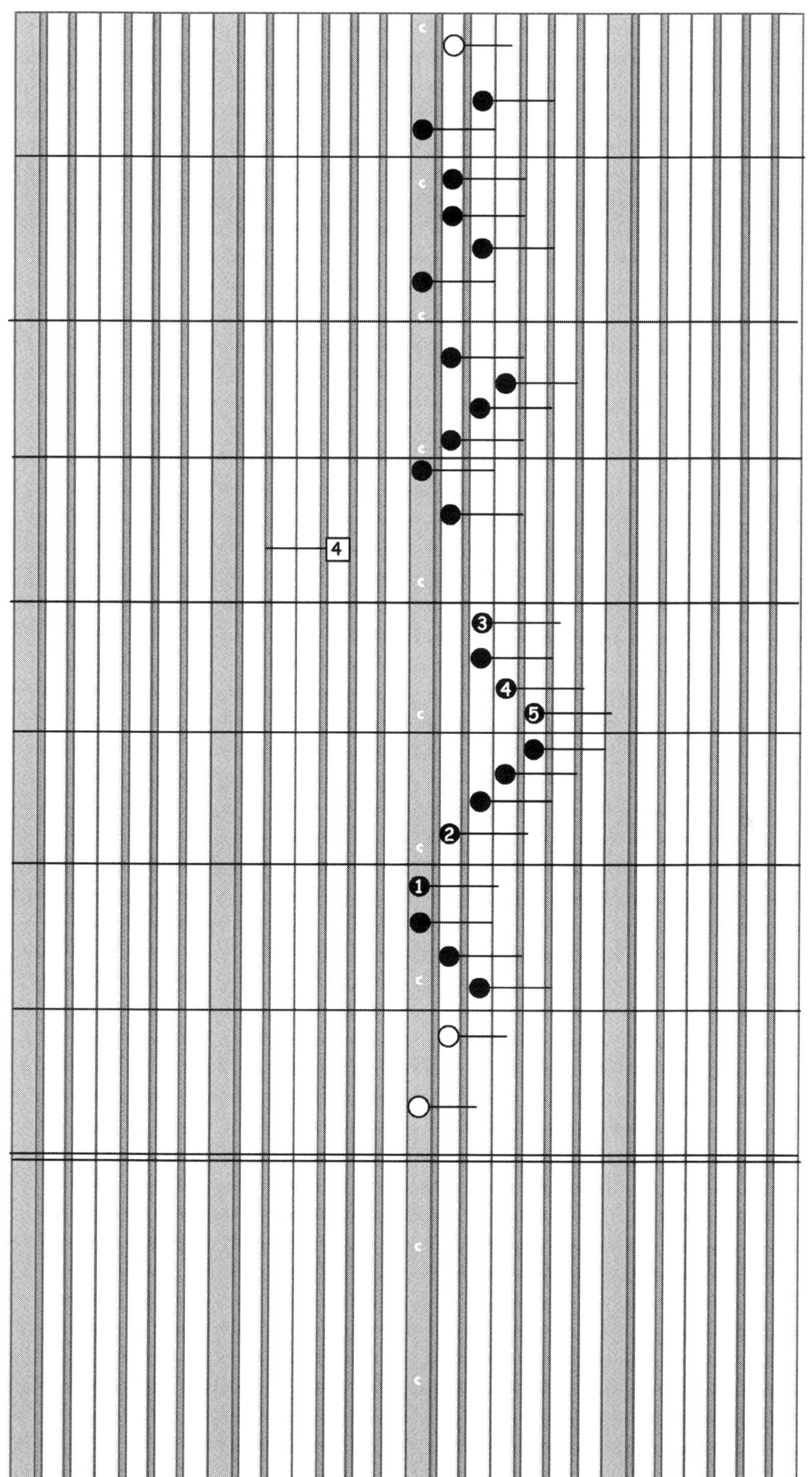

Ode to Joy - Version 4

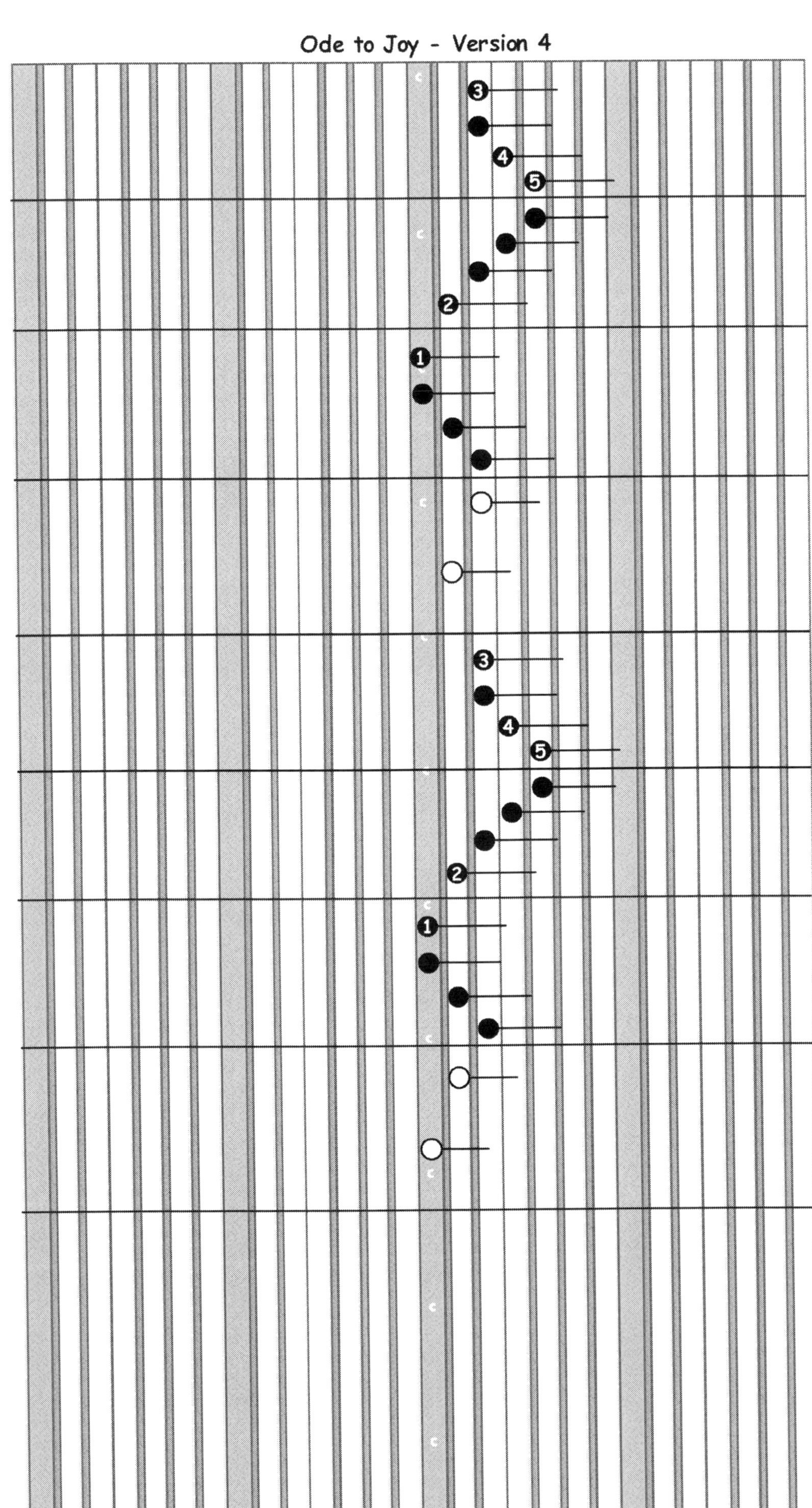

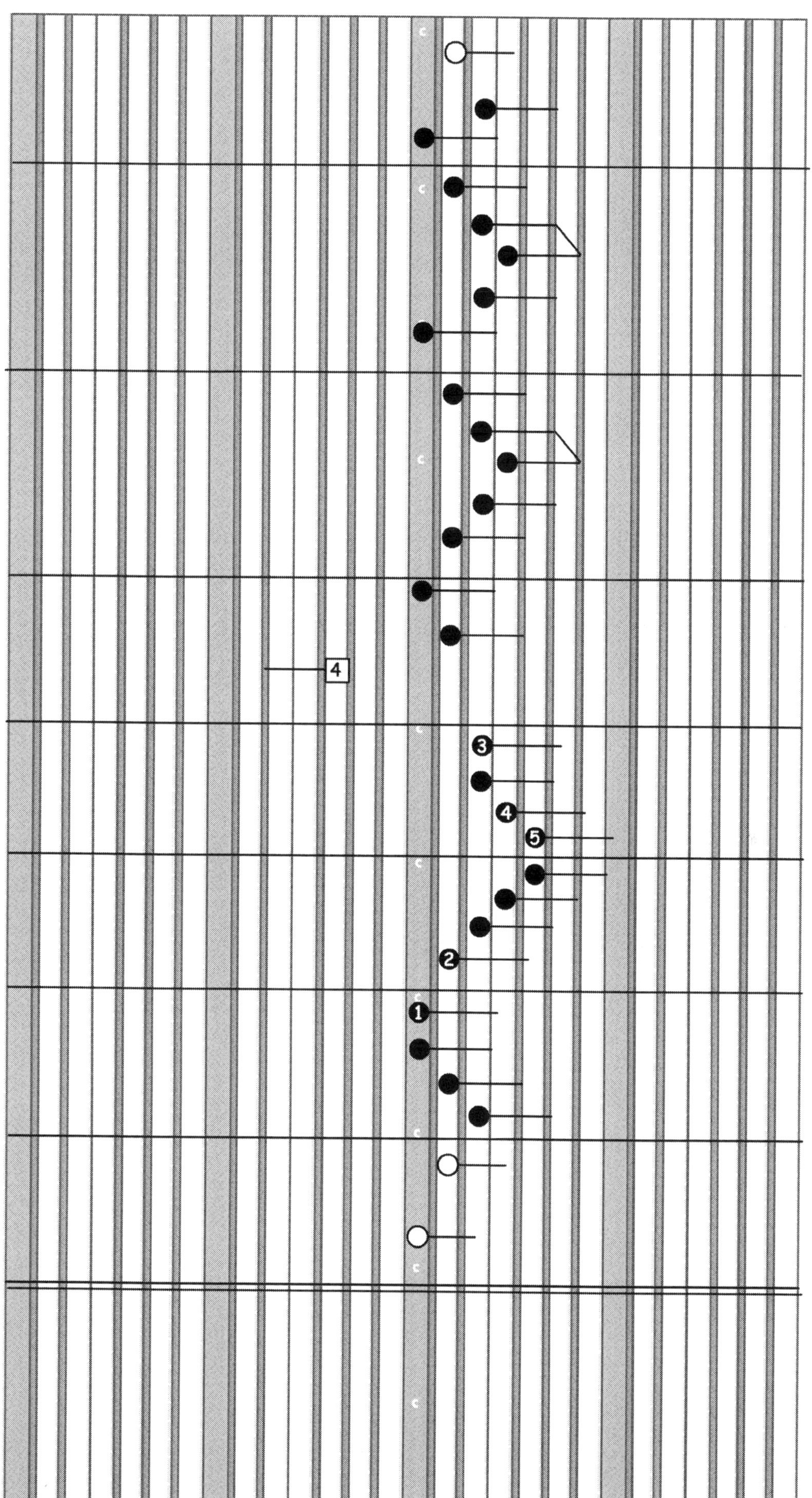

Ode to Joy - Version 5

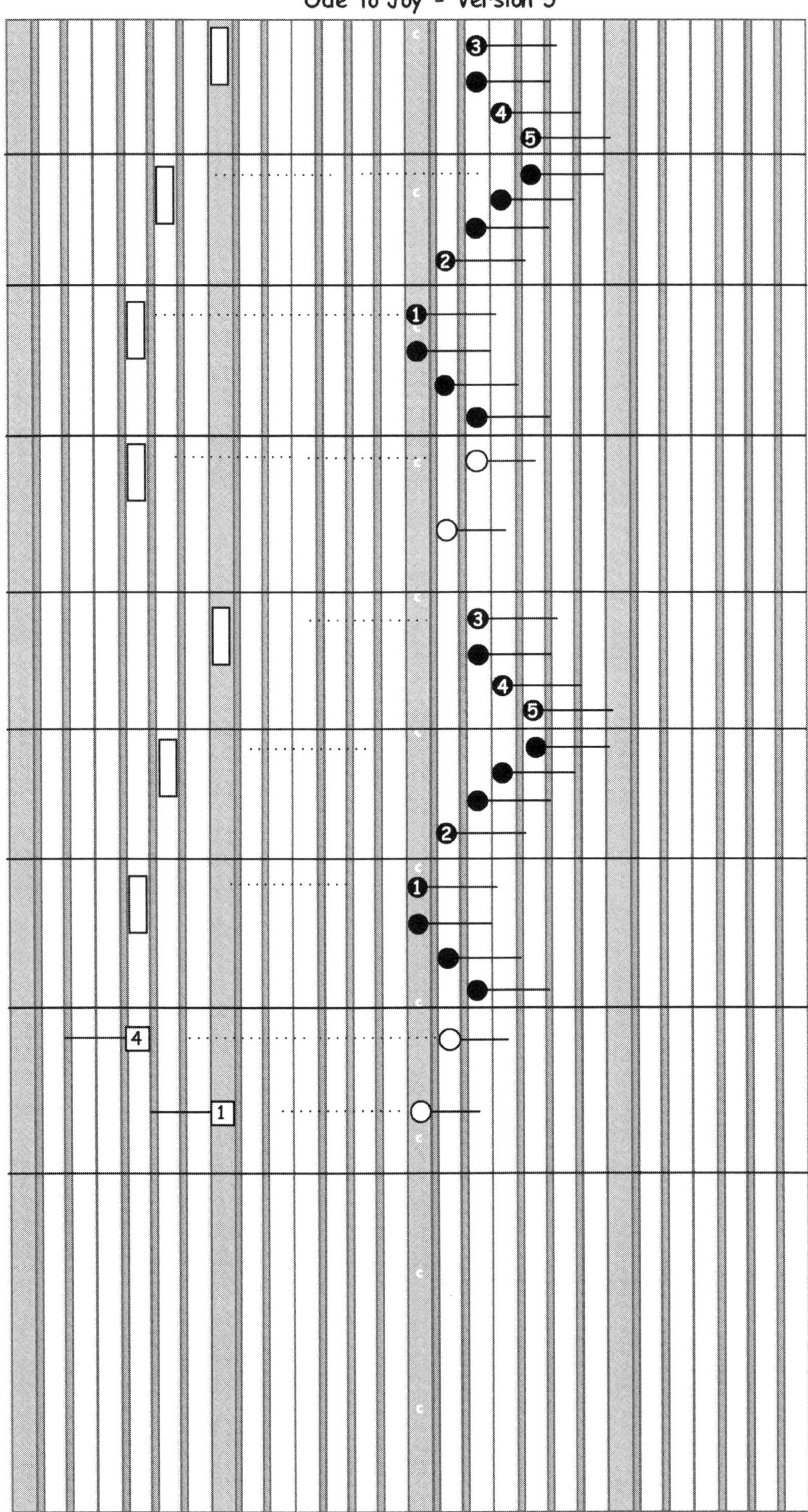

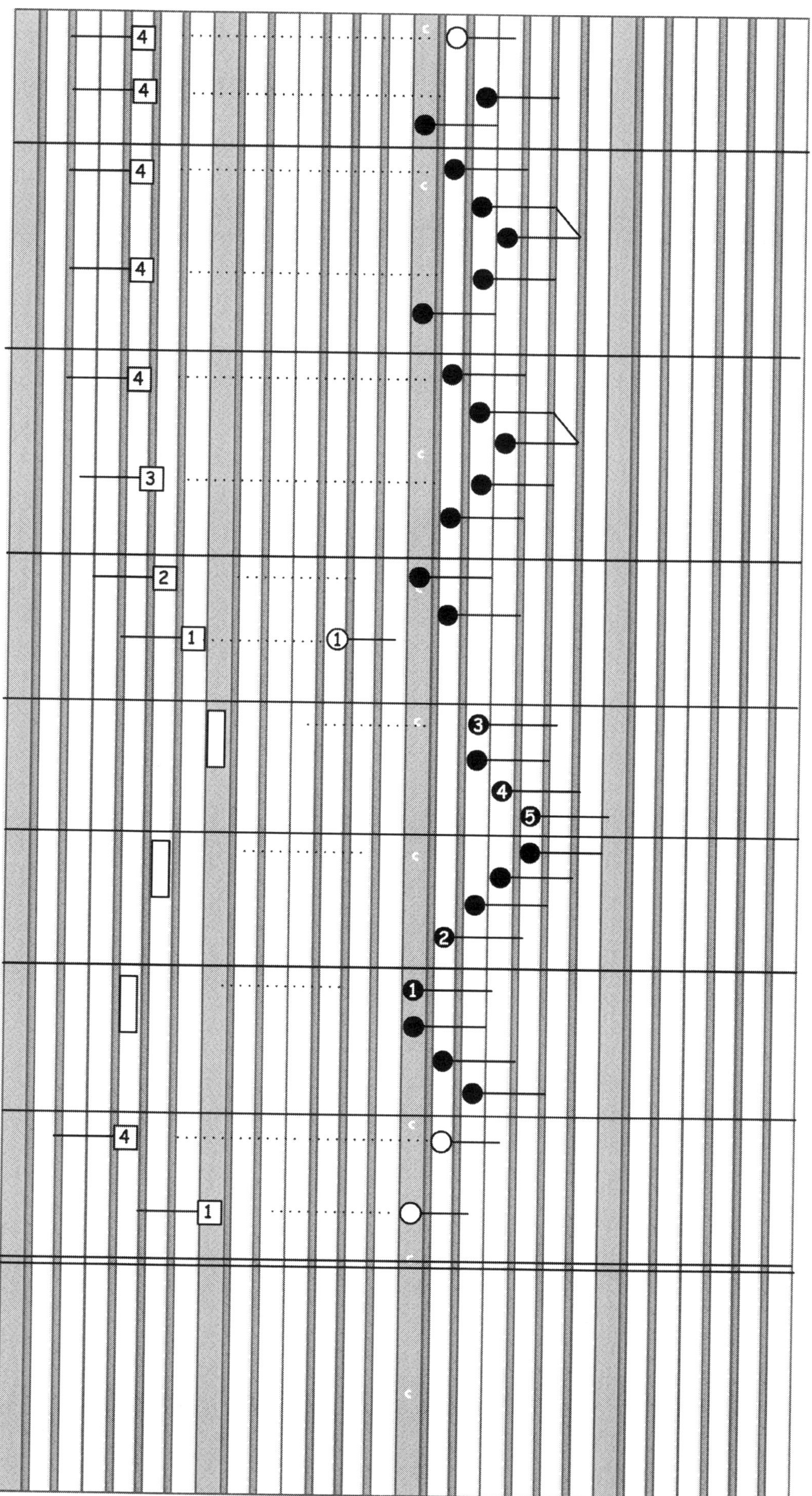

4
4
4
4
4
3
2
1
1
3
4
5
2
1
4
1

Ode to Joy - Version 6

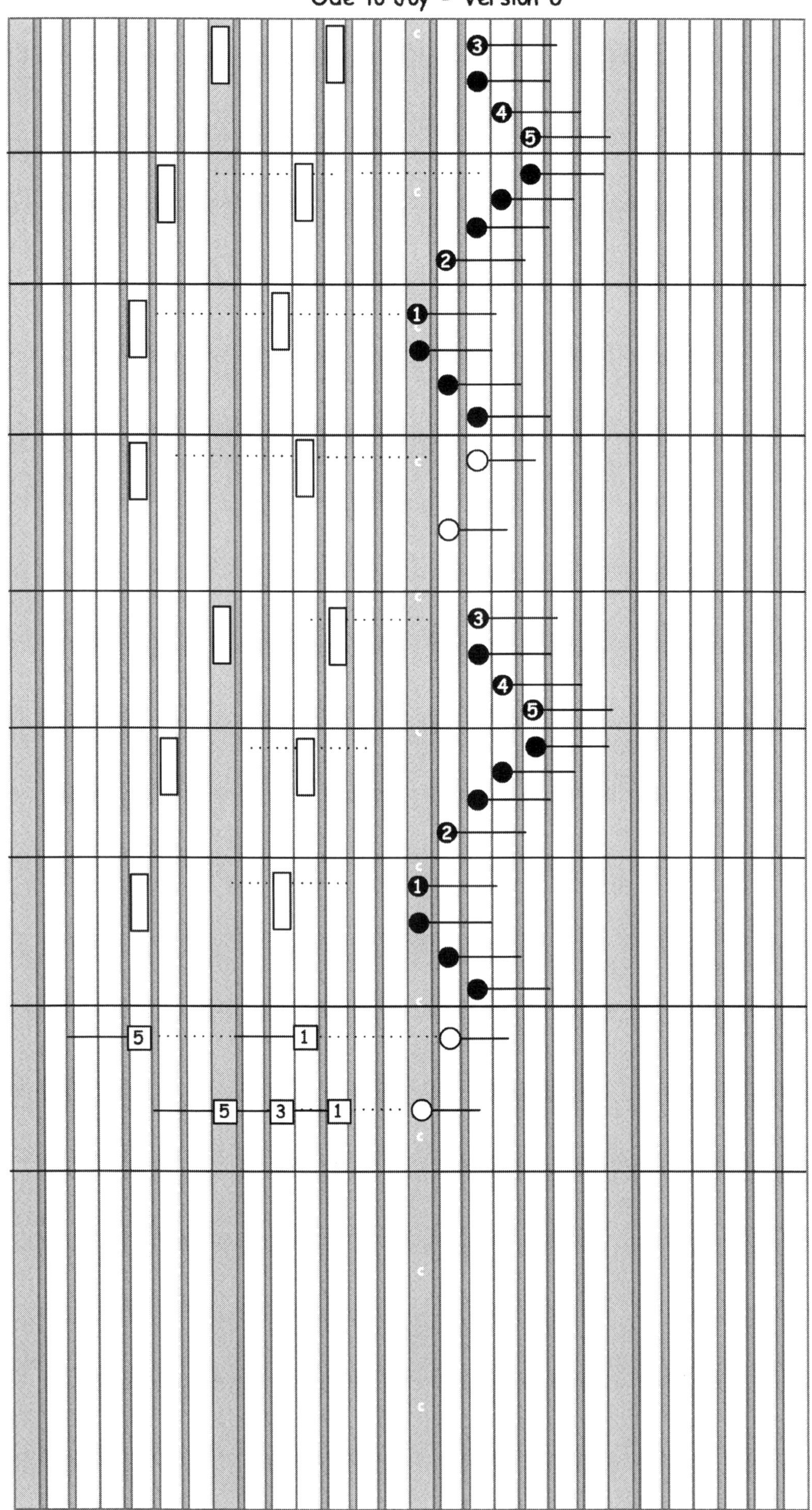

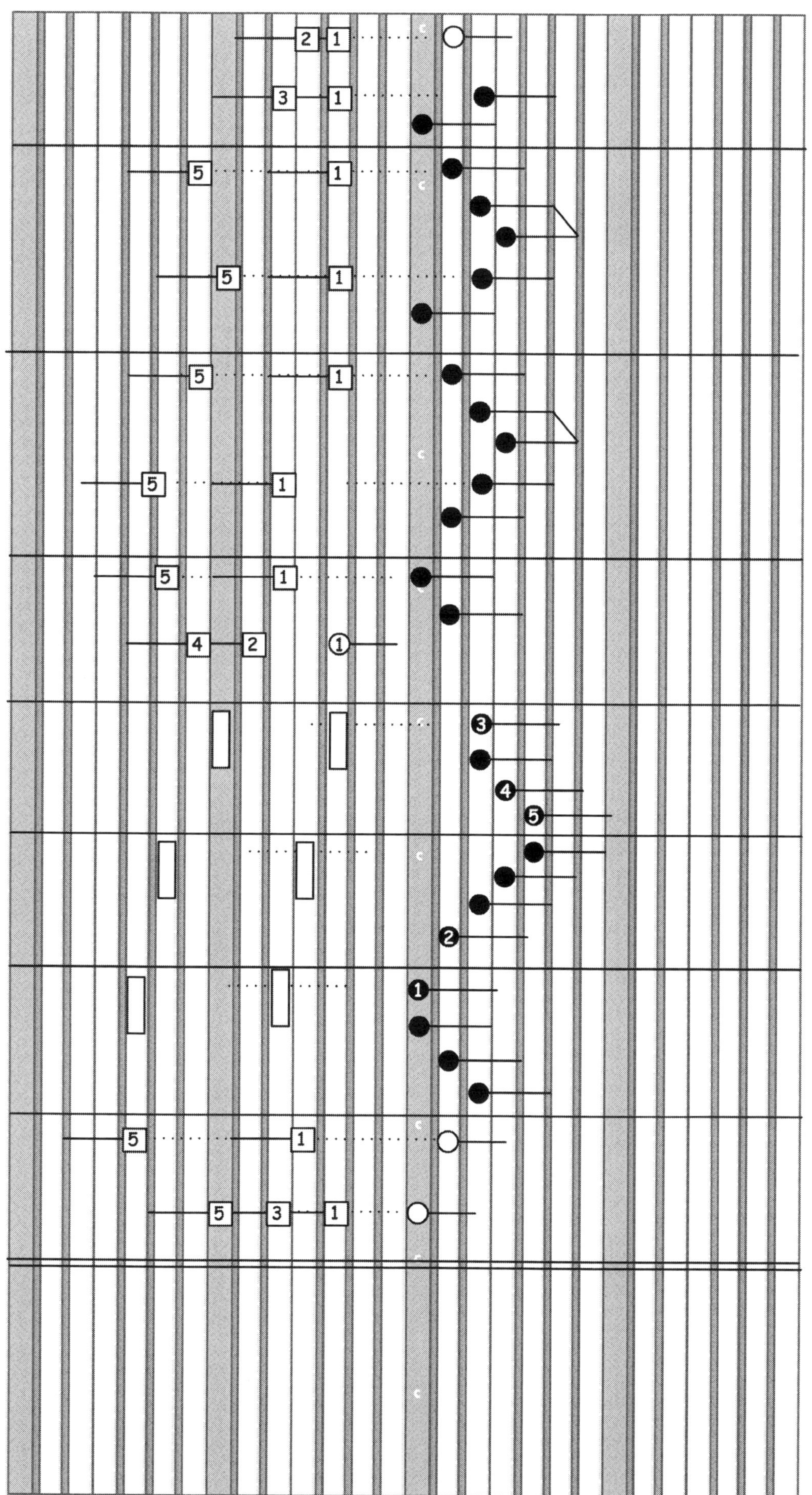

HOW TO PLAY "FUR ELISE"

Beethoven's Fur Elise is one of the most classic pieces to play on the piano. We include here the first part of it, which is played the most by beginner pianist all over the World. The second part becomes more difficult. What we include here is for sure the part that you've always wanted to play.

It is advisable to observe the suggested fingering on this piece. The notes have little or not difference with the original music part although we are starting to see here the rhythmical freedom that the Multiline system is trying to achieve.

We are mostly working on *Eighth* notes here, most of the time; therefore it could be a good idea to synchronize the pulse beat with every Eighth note rather than with every Quarter note that we have used with Ode to Joy. Once you mastered the piece you can go as fast as 200-metronome speed, with one Eighth note per beat.

When you encounter this indication:

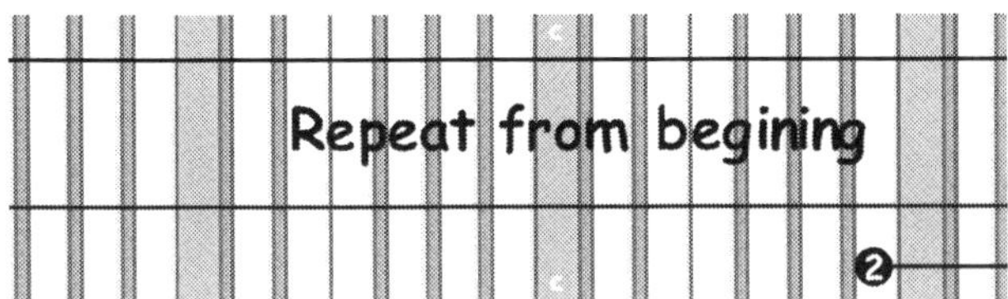

…as you must have guessed, start from the beginning and, when getting back to this point for second time, you then ignore it and carry on.

When you see this sign:

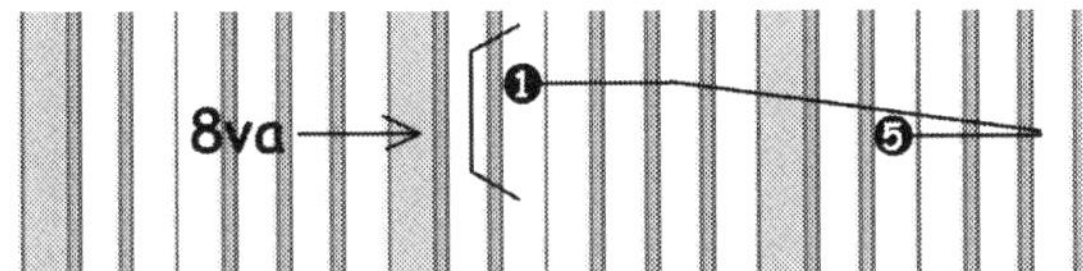

…it means that whatever is written has to be transposed seven white notes to the right. That affects in this case to the all the notes enclosed by the square bracket. We need this sign to write notes in the high pitch of the keyboard without having to represent every single note on the keyboard all the time in our Multiline paper.

Remember there are moments in which a last note of a series of notes on the right hand hammers at the same time to the first note of a set start playing on the left hand:

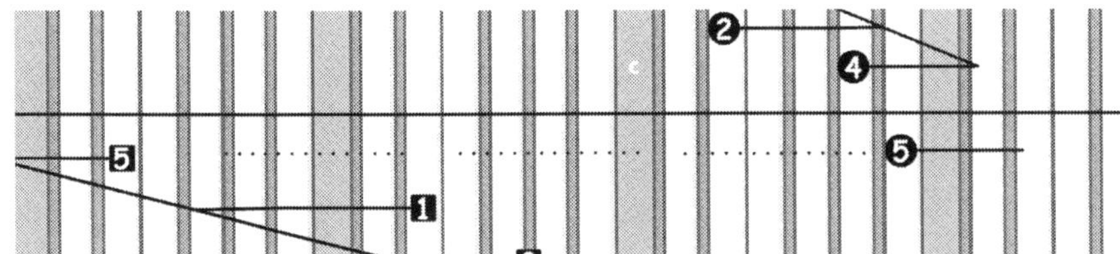

In order to help to identify these moments of simultaneity we link the notes with dotted lines.

FUR ELISE - L. v. Beethoven - (Fragment)

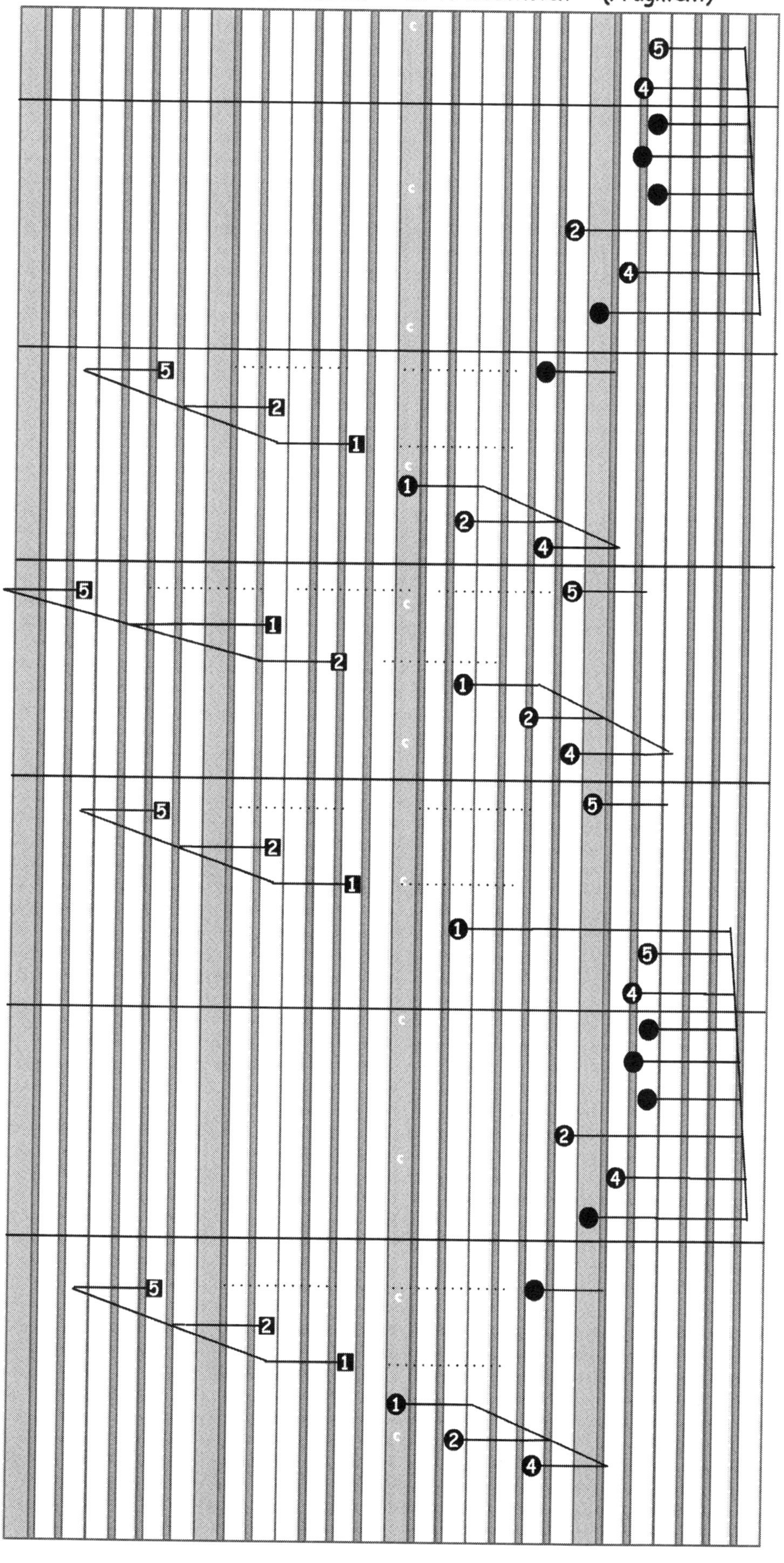

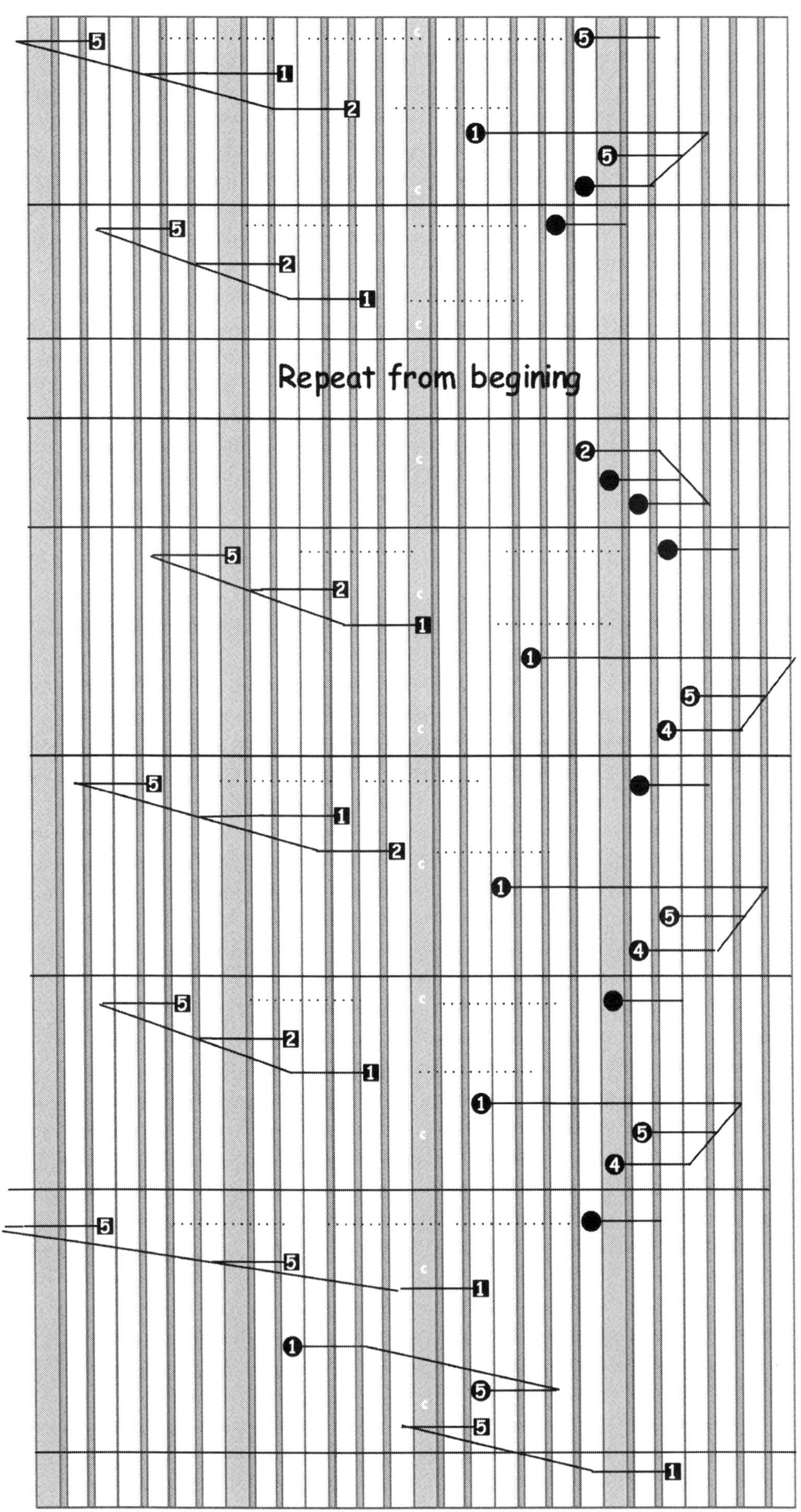
Repeat from begining

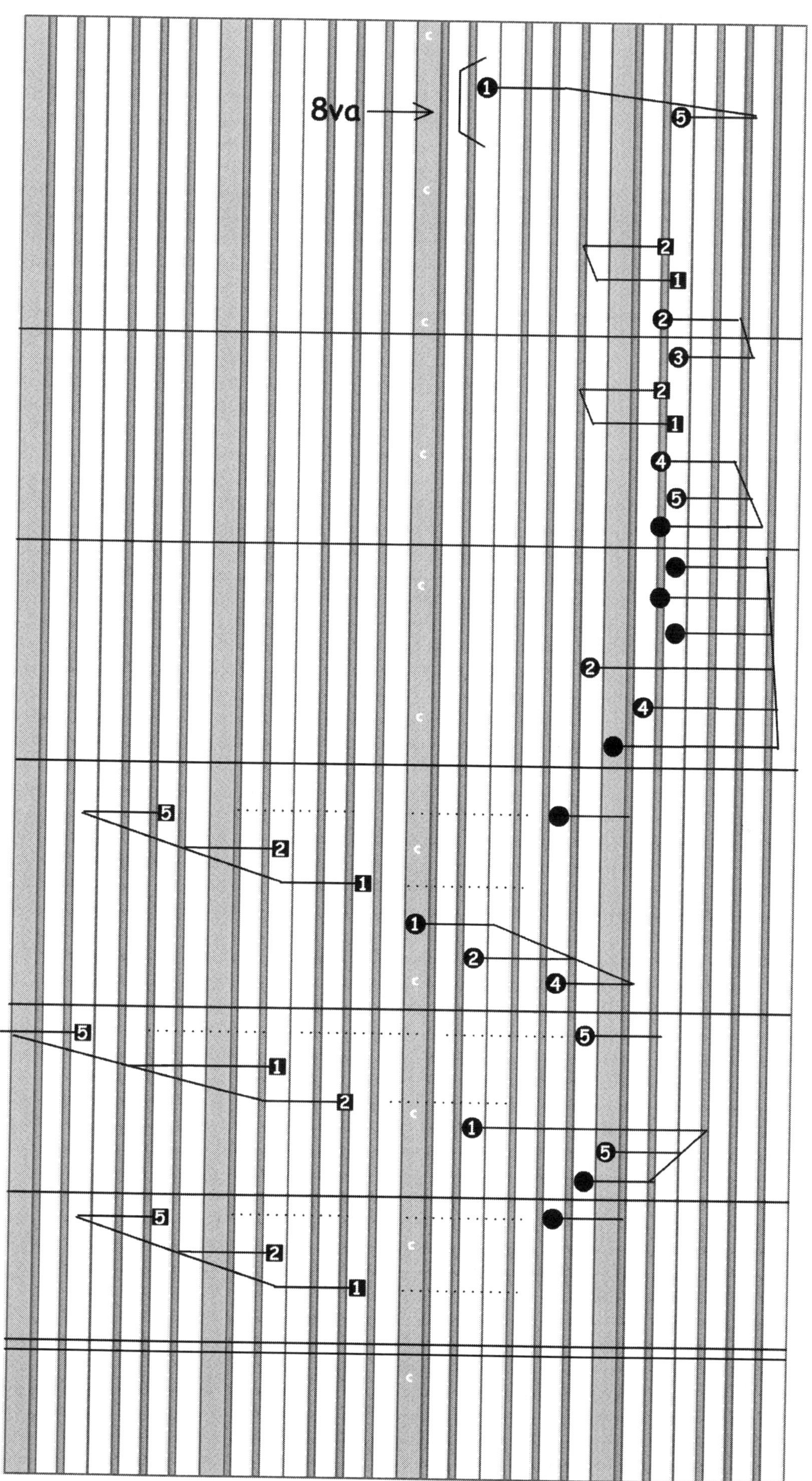
8va

HOW TO PLAY "BUNESSAN"

Better know as "Morning has broken" -thanks to the added poem to this traditional tune-, this piece help us to introduce a new sign to our set of symbols: We will call it *triangle* and it will add half of the duration of a whatever figure is followed by it. Take these Half notes with a triangle (know as dotted note in traditional notation):

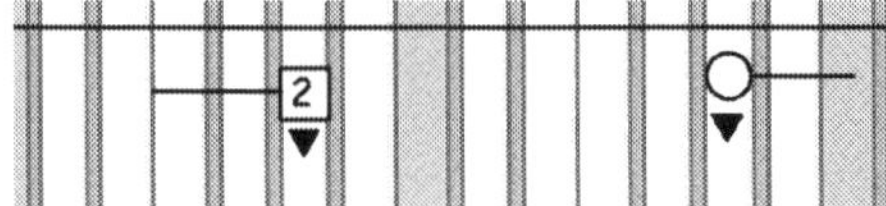

Typically, a half note will last two beats. Well, when affected by a triangle, we will add half of the duration to it. Half of two is one, two plus one is three. **A triangled half note will last three beats** instead of two. This make sense if you see a triangled Half on the left hand confronted with three Quarters on the right hand:

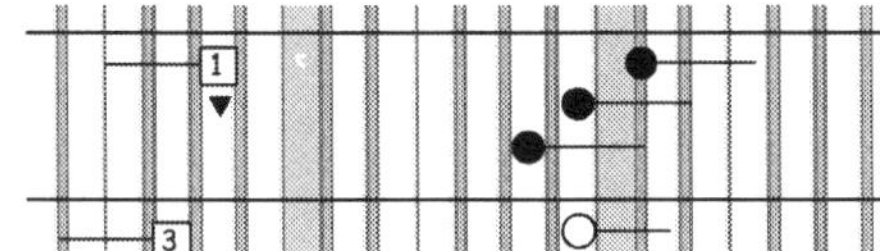

You can see here how a triangled Half note lasts for as long as three Quarters.
We take as a unit a Quarter, as we did in the Ode to Joy, this is, a Quarter per beat.
When we have three *Quarters* on the right hand and a triangled half on the left, just let the right hand take the lead and you will know when to strike the next note on the left hand.
When both, the right and left hand are doing triangled halves, count three mentally, always following the speed of the pulse you've chosen to play the piece.

When you see that two triangled half notes are tied together like in here:

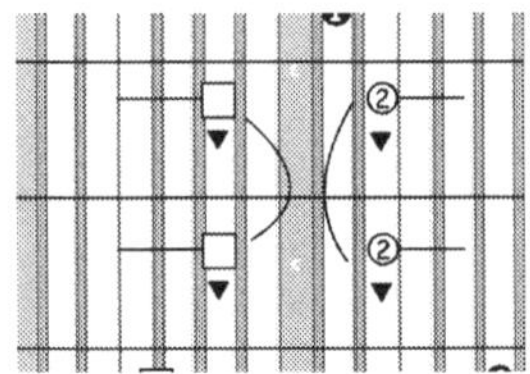

…make sure you keep both hands pressing the indicated keys for the space of six beats (3+3). In other situation like here:

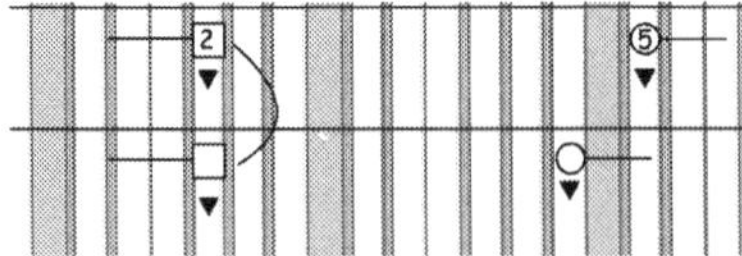

…the left hand presses the key for six beats whilst the right hand every three.

THE TWO VERSIONS OF BUNESSAN

We've included two versions of Bunessan. The second version is slightly harder as it plays two simultaneous notes on the left hand. Play the one that you find more suitable to your availability of time and energy, or perhaps one after the other.

HOW TO PLAY BACH'S PRELUDE IN C

This prelude is another of the classic pieces for piano beginners. It is the first prelude of the Well Tempered Clavier Book I written by Bach. Although dated 1722, it still sounds like it was written in modern times. Every single note here observes Bach's original part.

We set as the rhythmical unit the usual Quarter note, so we will play a Quarter for every beat. The ideal speed for this piece would sit around the number 176 of your metronome. Start slower until you feel comfortable at that speed.

Repeat every box twice except for the last three where indicated "stop repeating". Every box is delimited by horizontal bars.

You'll see curvy lines on the notes played by the left hand, like ties that connect with nothing:

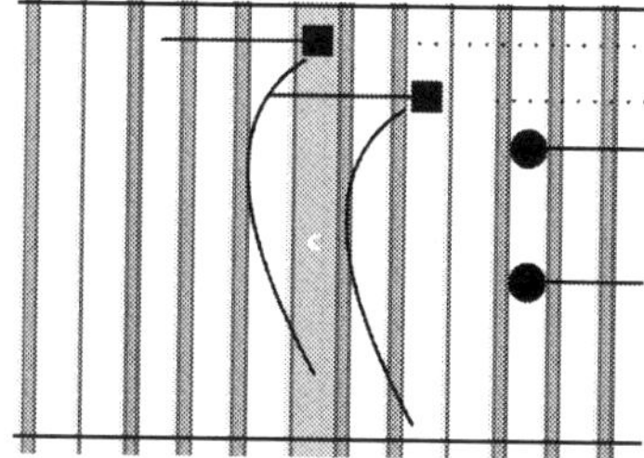

That means that we will keep those notes pressed until we arrive to the next box. The musical jargon for this is "let it ring". If you are using the *sustain* pedal lift it and press it again every time you cross the horizontal division bar to prevent the sounds from becoming mushy.

Bunessan (Morning has Broken) - Version 1

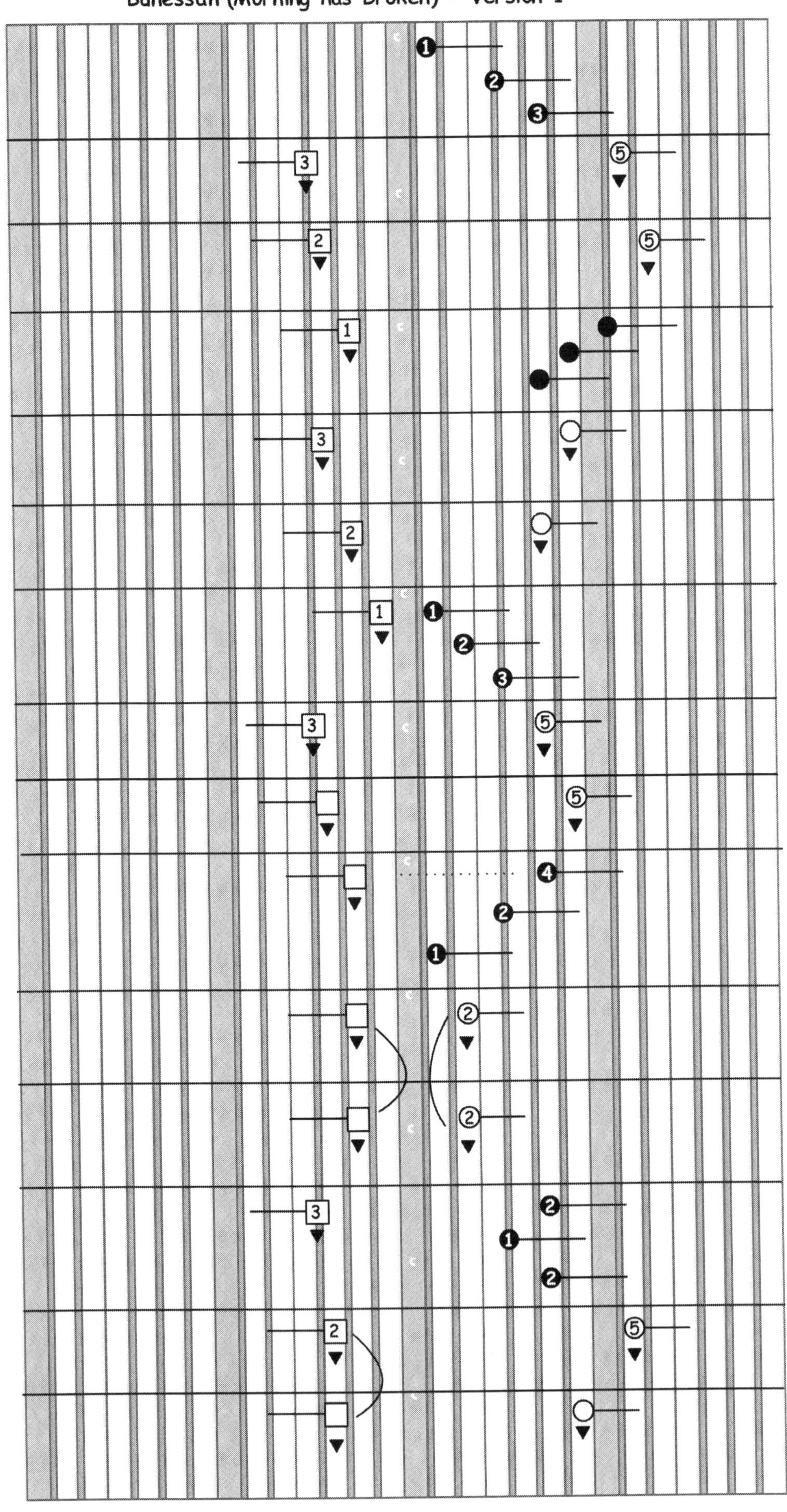

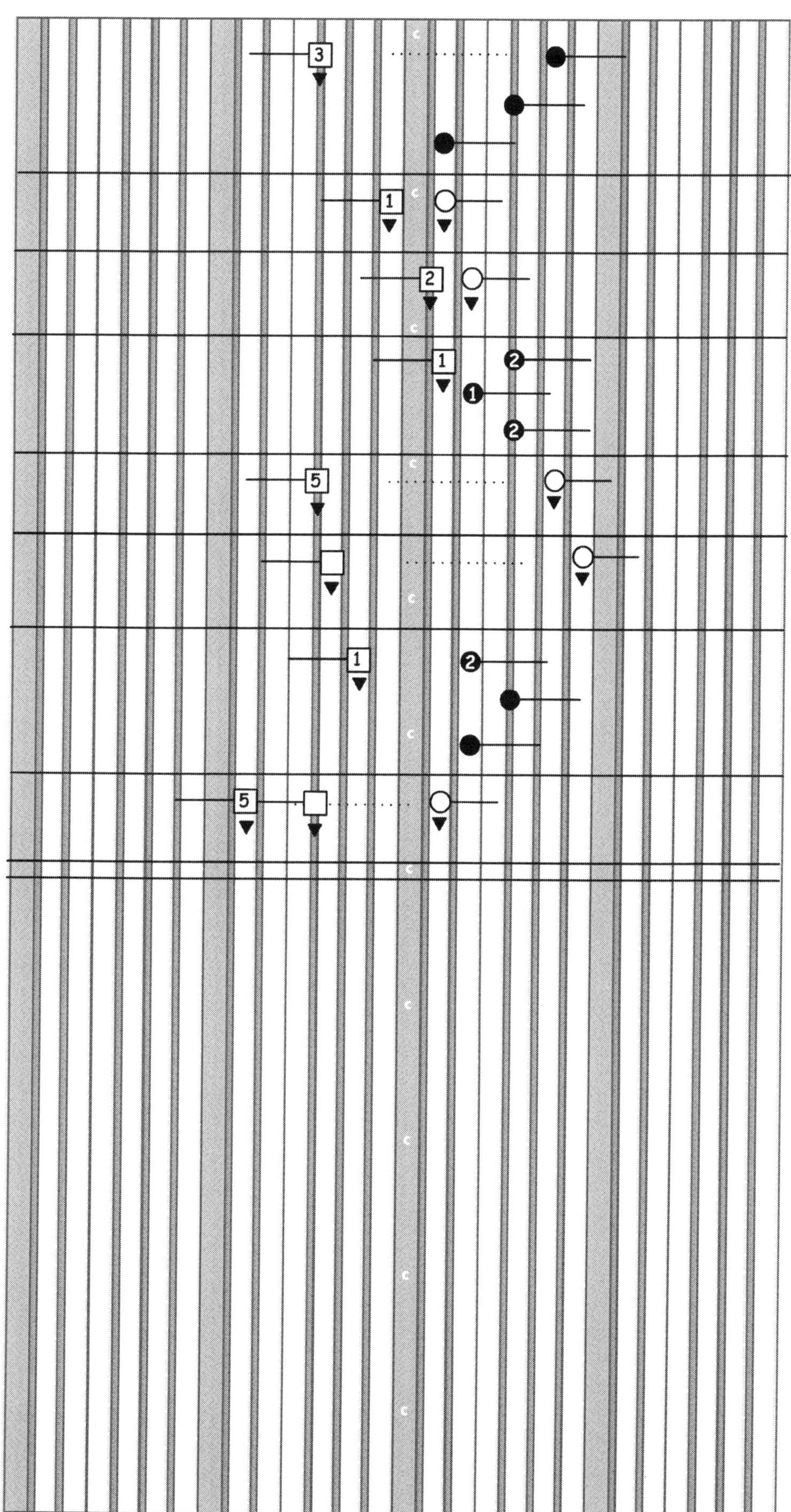

Bunessan (Morning has Broken) - Version 2

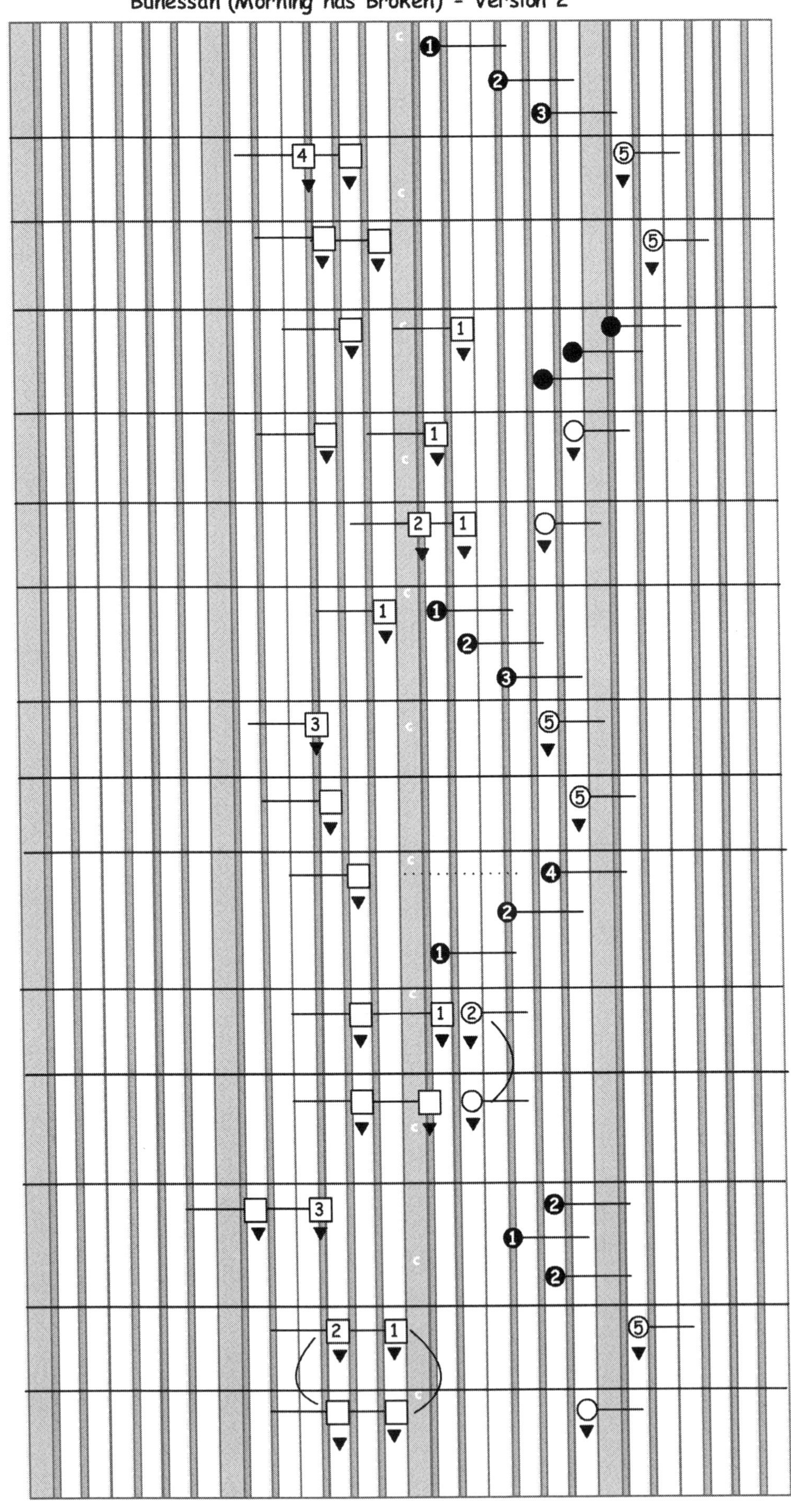

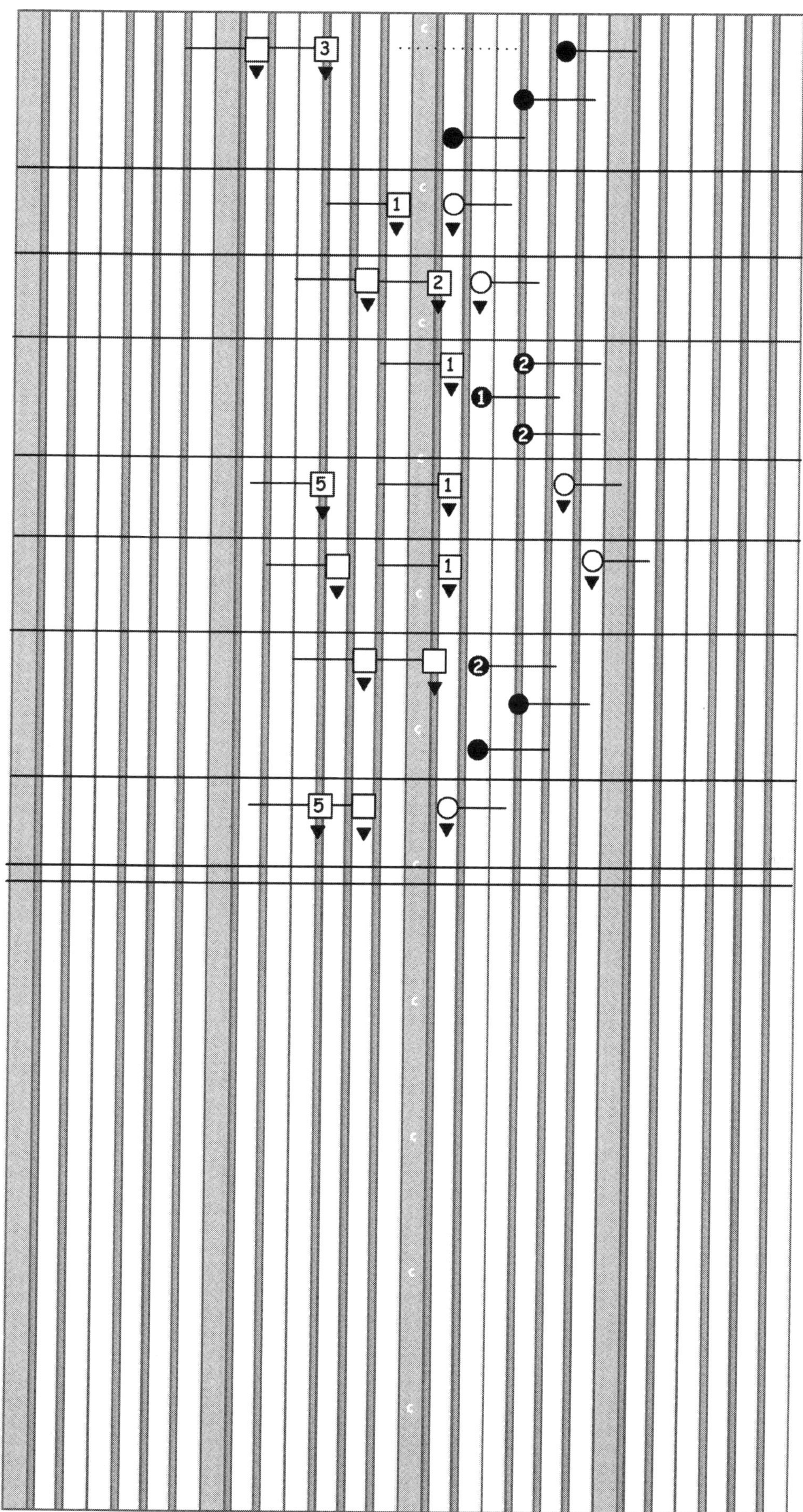

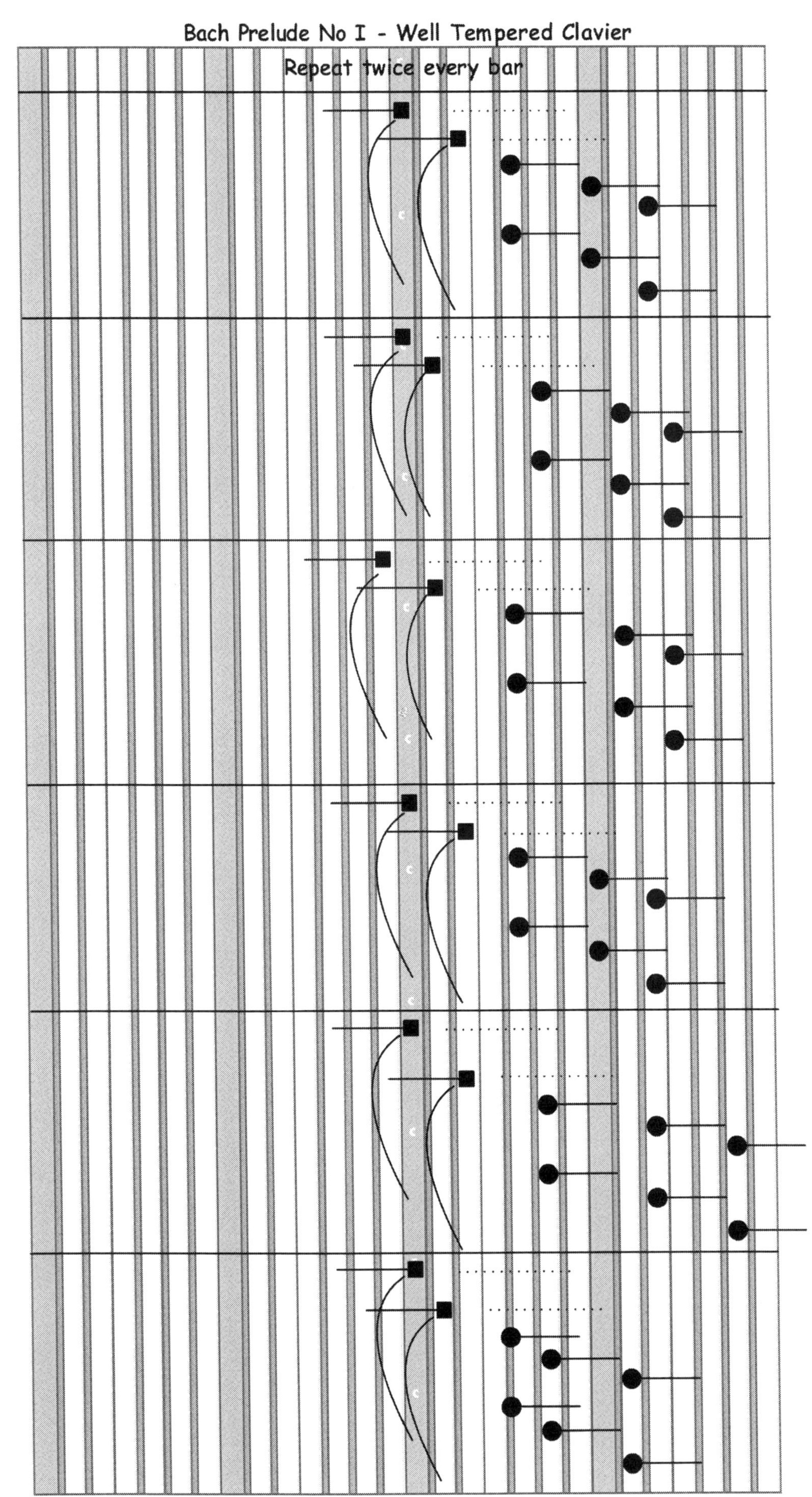
Bach Prelude No I - Well Tempered Clavier
Repeat twice every bar

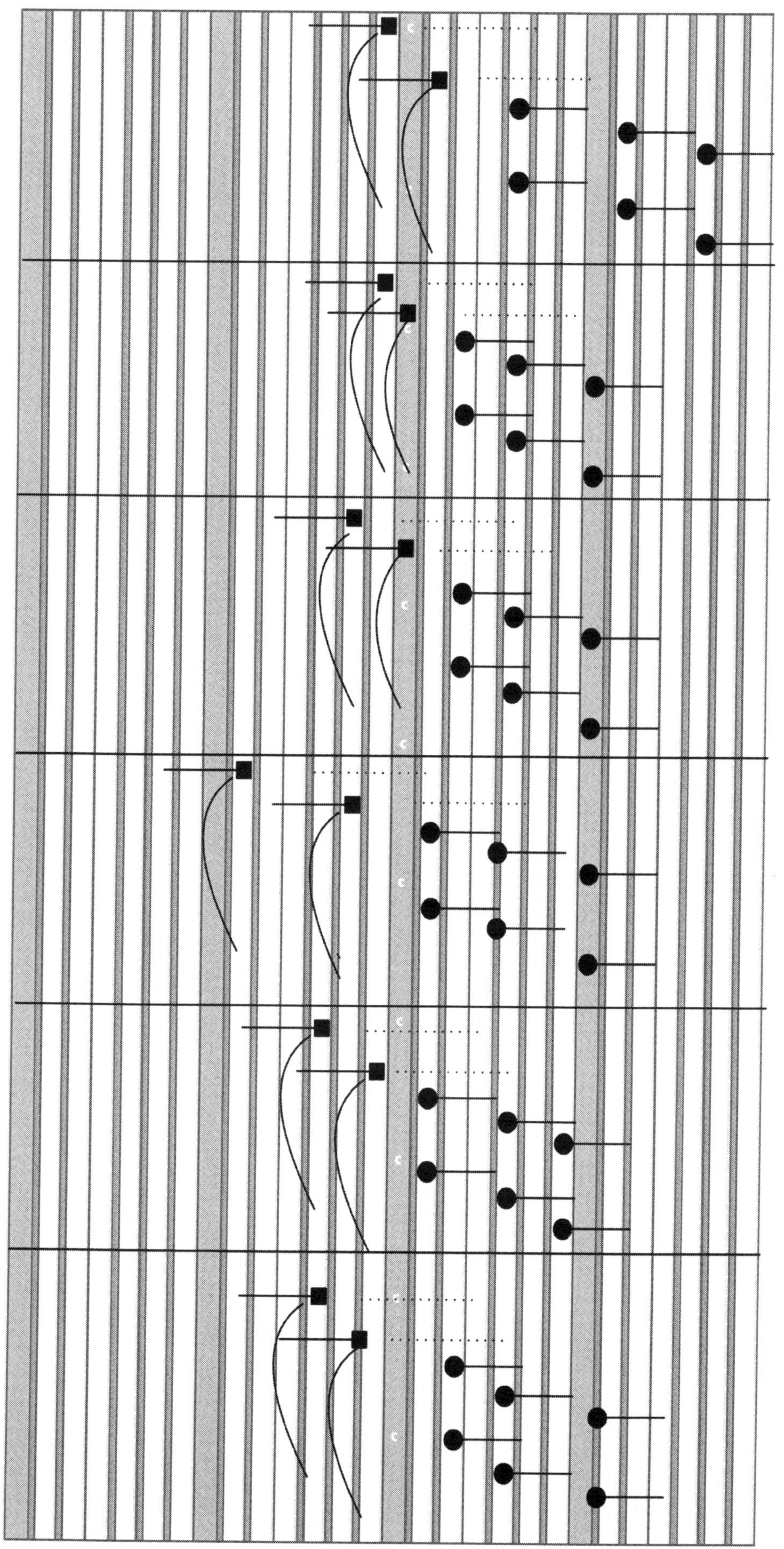

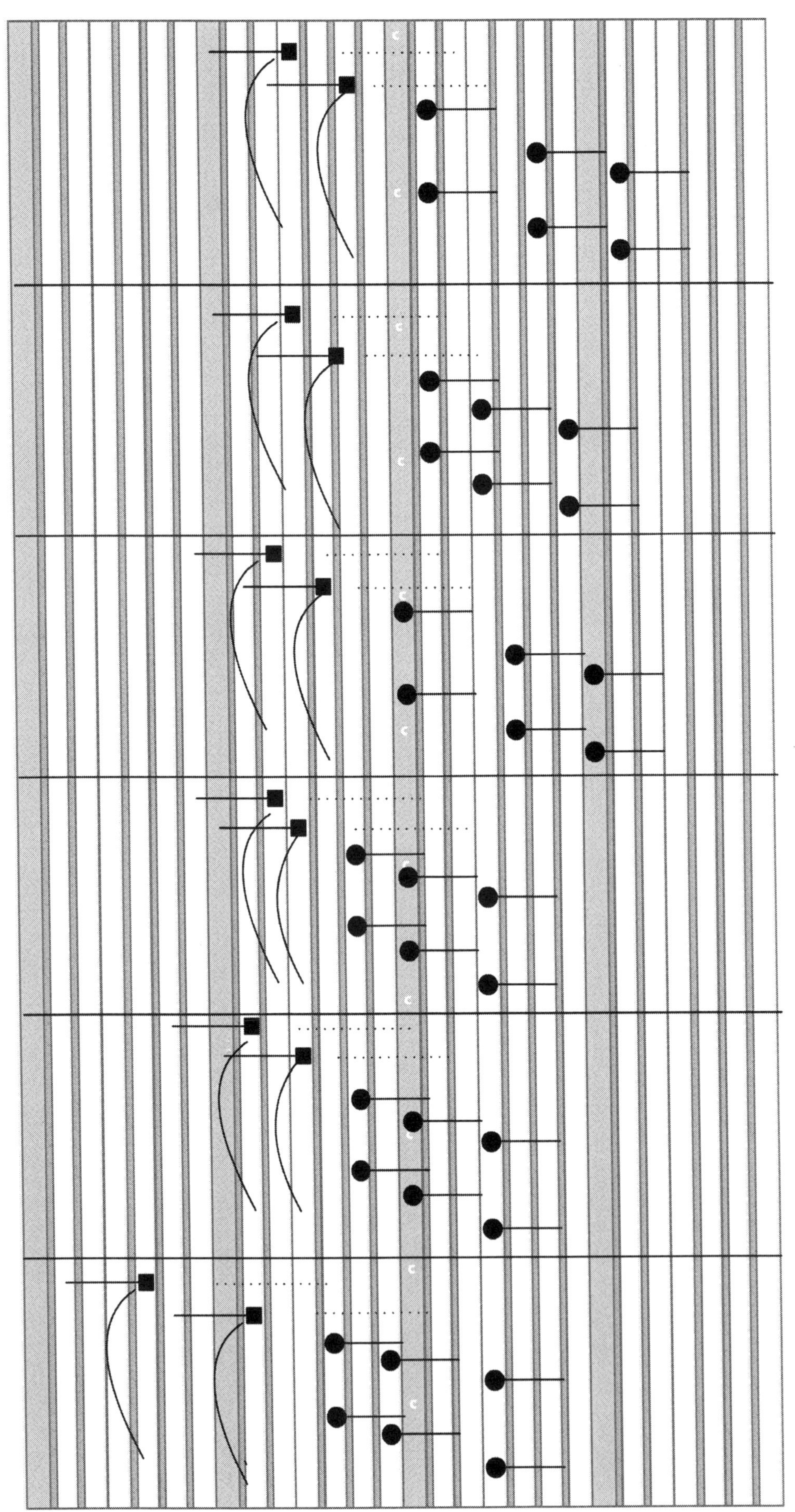

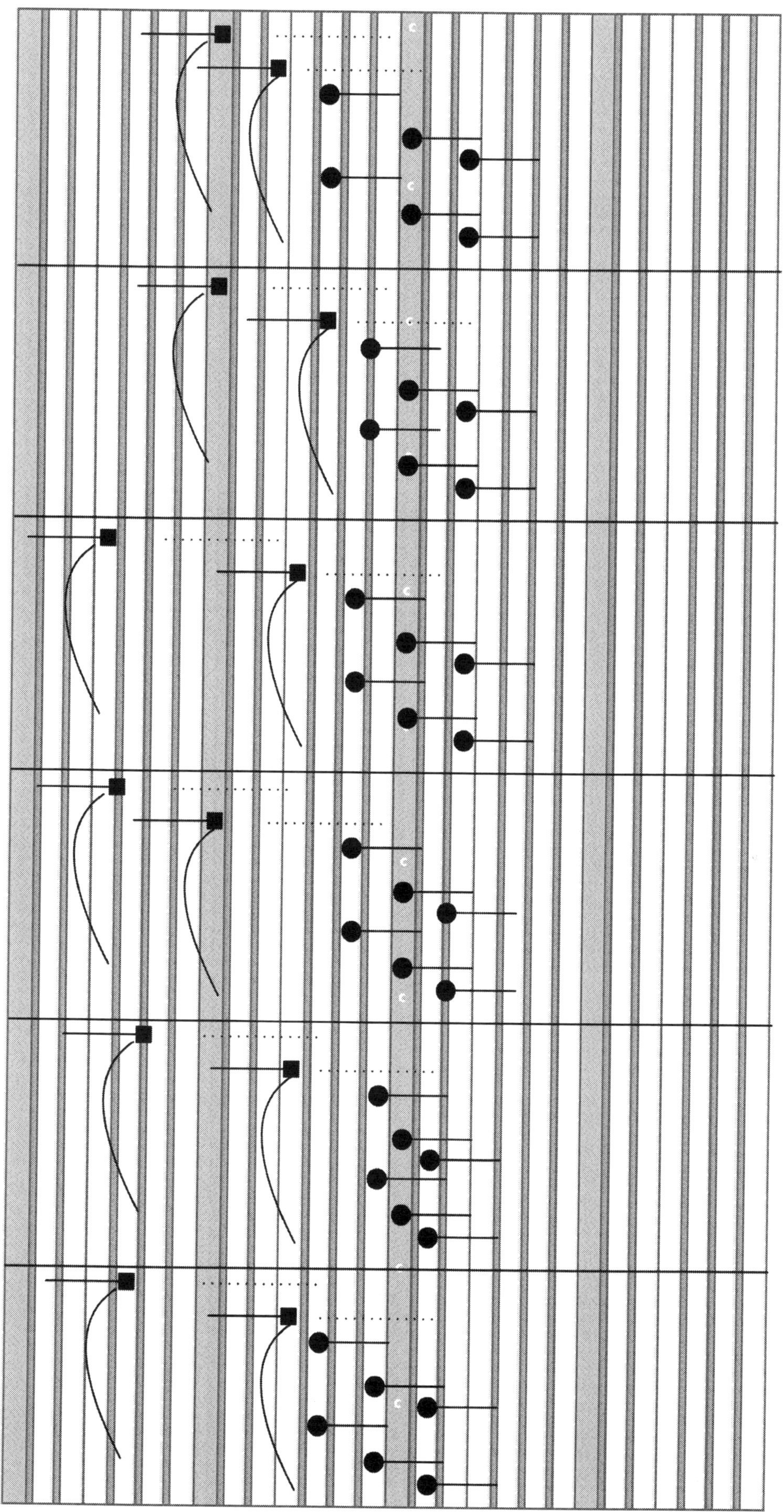

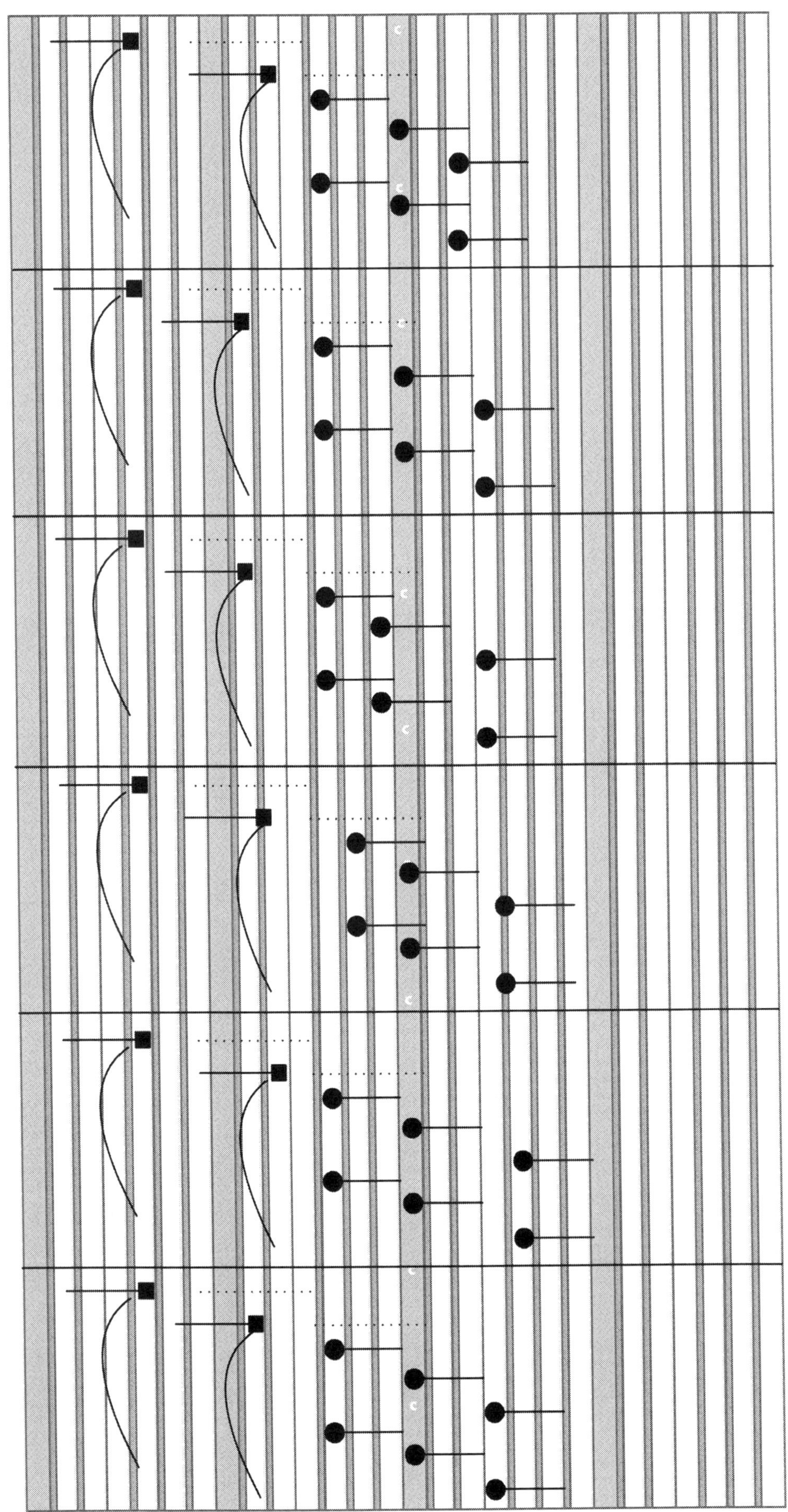

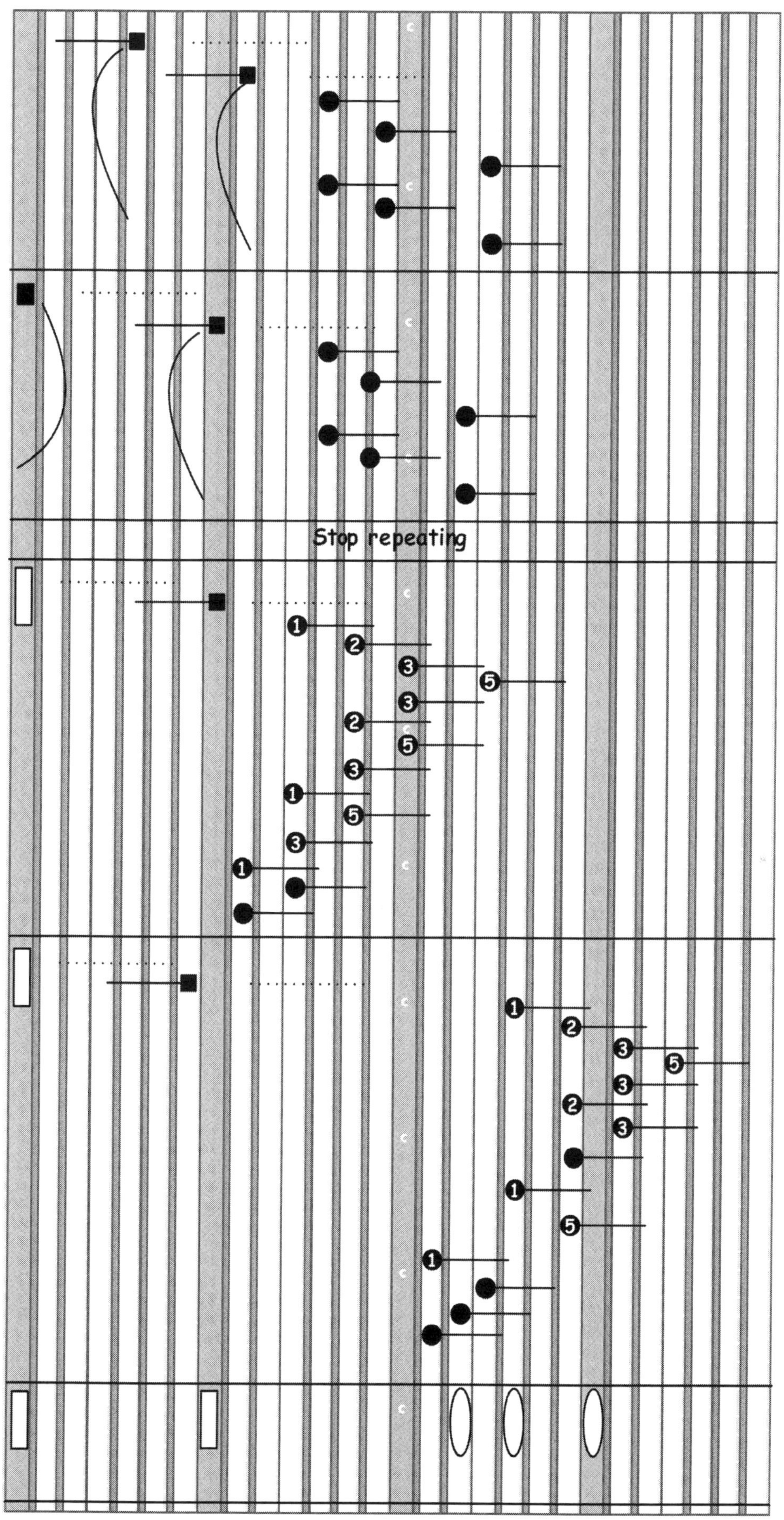
Stop repeating

HOW TO PLAY AULD LANG SYNE

This traditional farewell song employs a very well used rhythmical cell, a triangled Quarter followed by an Eighth note and another two Quarters afterwards:

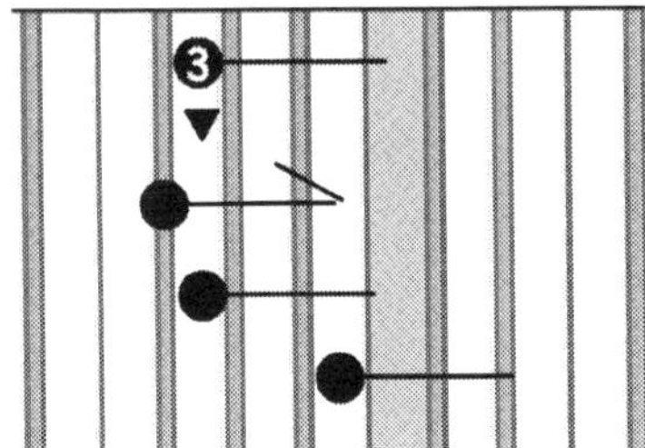

Here the Quarter note is extended by half of its value for being affected by the triangle. That will leave us with a shorter space to play the second note which, in consequence, we will reduce to an Eighth note if we want the following Quarter to coincide with the third beat. This way we can continue observing *the one-Quarter-per-beat deal*.

Another way to approach this issue is to count from one to four making sure every number coincides with a beat: *one-two-three-four*. We then add an "and" between the two and the three: *one-two and-three-four*. Then the first note will match the word "one", the second the word "and", the third the word three and the fourth the word "four". The rhythmical cell like this created will sound like saying "roaast pata-to".

After all these attempts to explain with words what could be easily explained with music, we suggest you to listen to some versions of Auld Lang Syne and you'll grab the concept of the rhythm you have to follow on the right hand when you play this traditional Scottish tune.

We include two versions of the tune, being the second one slightly more challenging for the left hand as it employs two and many time three simultaneous notes as the right hand goes on with the melody.

HOW TO PLAY SCARBOROUGH FAIR

To play Scarborough Fair we need to think of a structure of three beats, this is, we mentally count 1-2-3-1-2-3-1-2-3- etc observing the speed of the pulse. We see that on the left hand there is a rhythmical pattern that repeats and only stops at the last bar. Although the notes change continuously, this is the pattern:

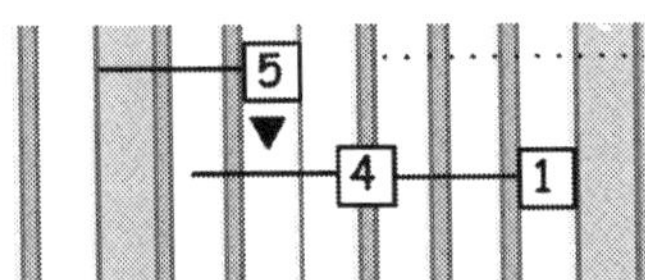

In this case, the triangled note will sound when we mentally say "one" -the first beat of the bar-, the other two half notes -non triangled- will sound when we mentally say two –the second beat of the bar. We keep the keys press until the following "one".

We also find an "X" like this one:

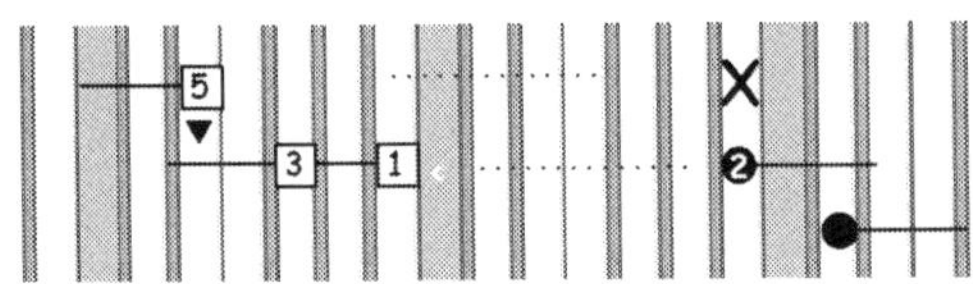

These are rests. In this case we don't play on the right hand but we still fill the space of a beat with "inactivity". In example above, the right hand does not play anything on the first beat of the bar, but it plays a note on the second and third beat. In the following example, the right hand does nothing on the first and second beat, but plays on the third beat.

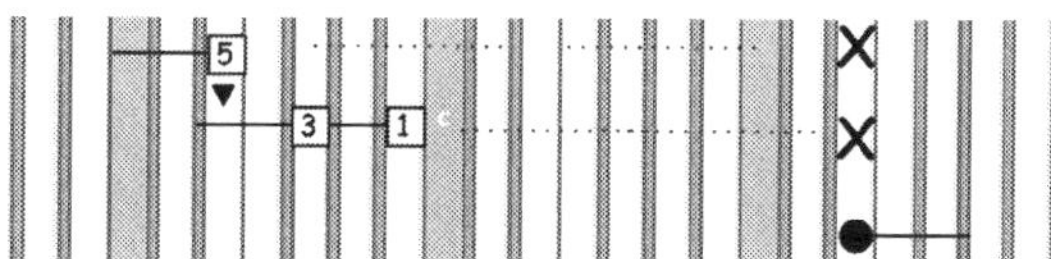

An ideal pulse speed for this tune would be 100 in metronome speed, although we can start slower in practice mode.

HOW TO PLAY GYMNOPEDIE

The indications for playing Scarborough Fair apply also for most of Gymnopedie. Counting 1-2-3-1-2-3… will helps us to keep up with the rhythm, although a metronome speed of 80 would be the ideal. As in Scarborough Fair, the left hand is dominated by a patter *note-chord*: a note on the first bit, a chord on the second.

A piece of music contained between bar like this…

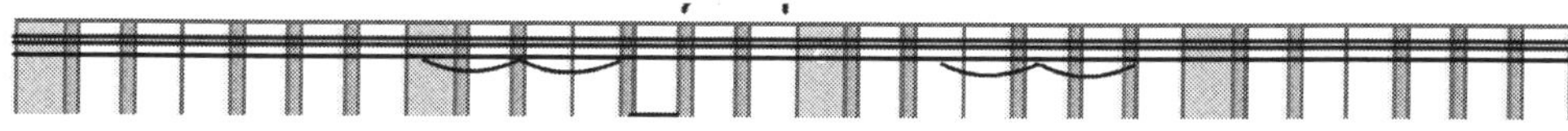

…and this…

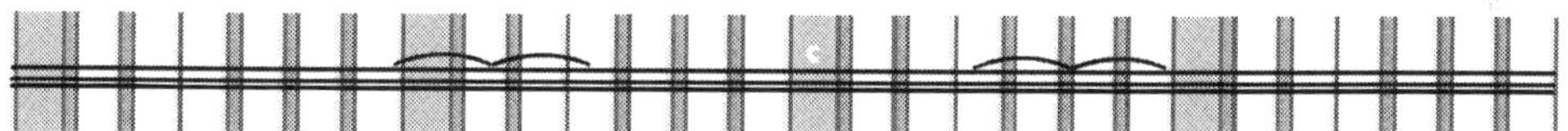

…is to be repeated twice.

Lastly at the last page we find a tie the one shown below:

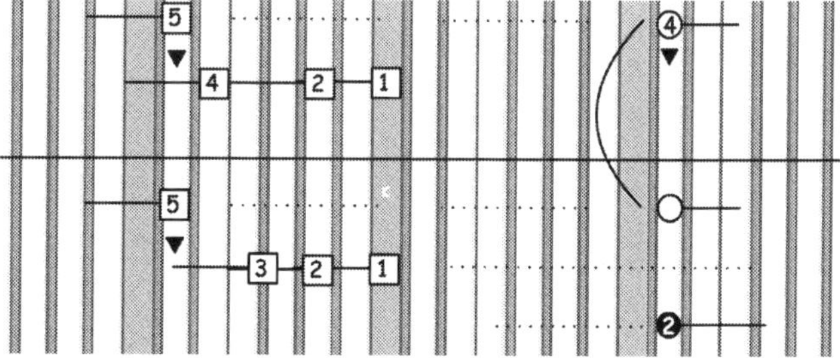

In this case keep the right hand fourth finger pressed for five beats.

Auld Lang Syne - Version 1- Arrangement: Marcello Palace

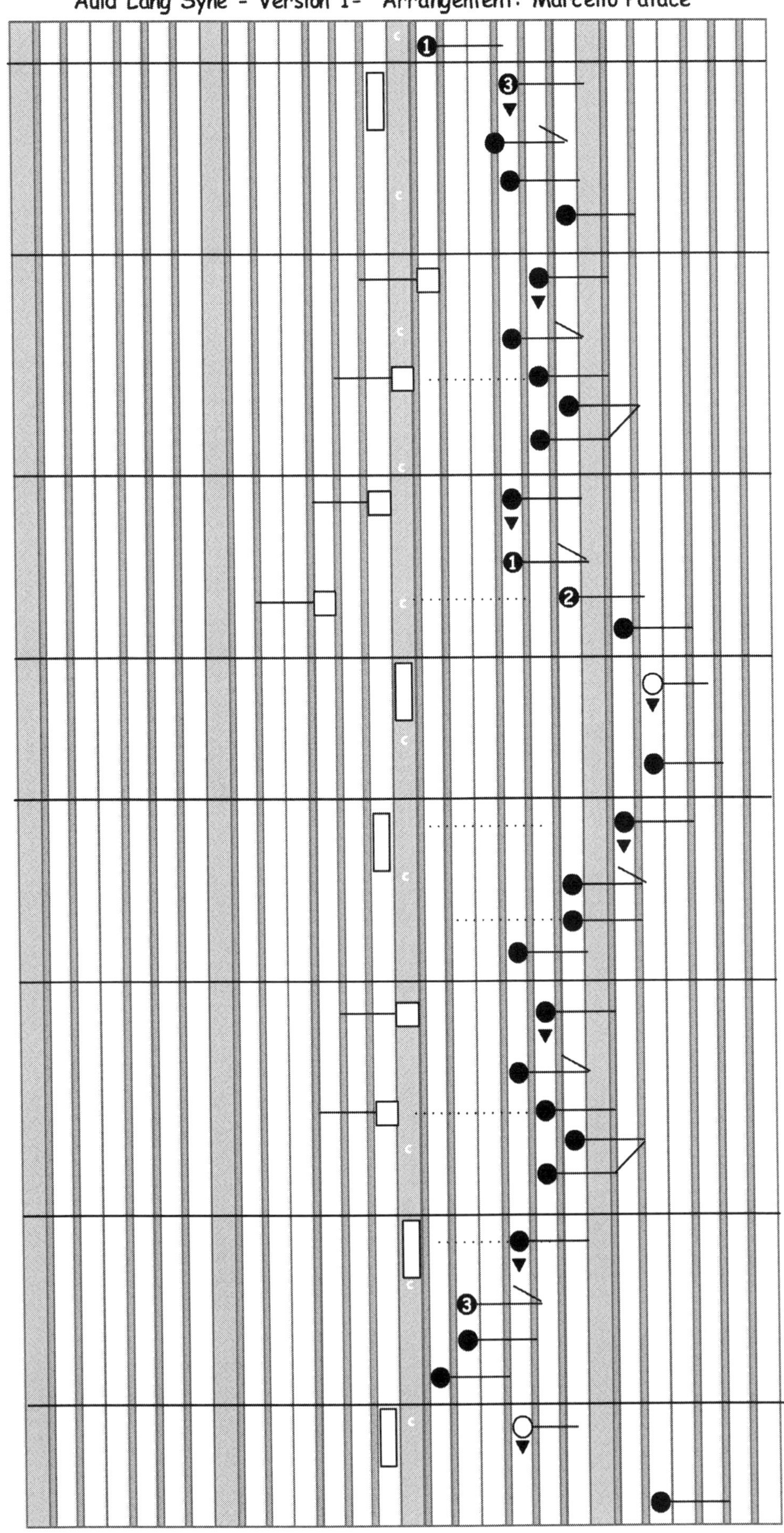

Auld Lang Syne -Version 2- Arrangement: Marcello Palace

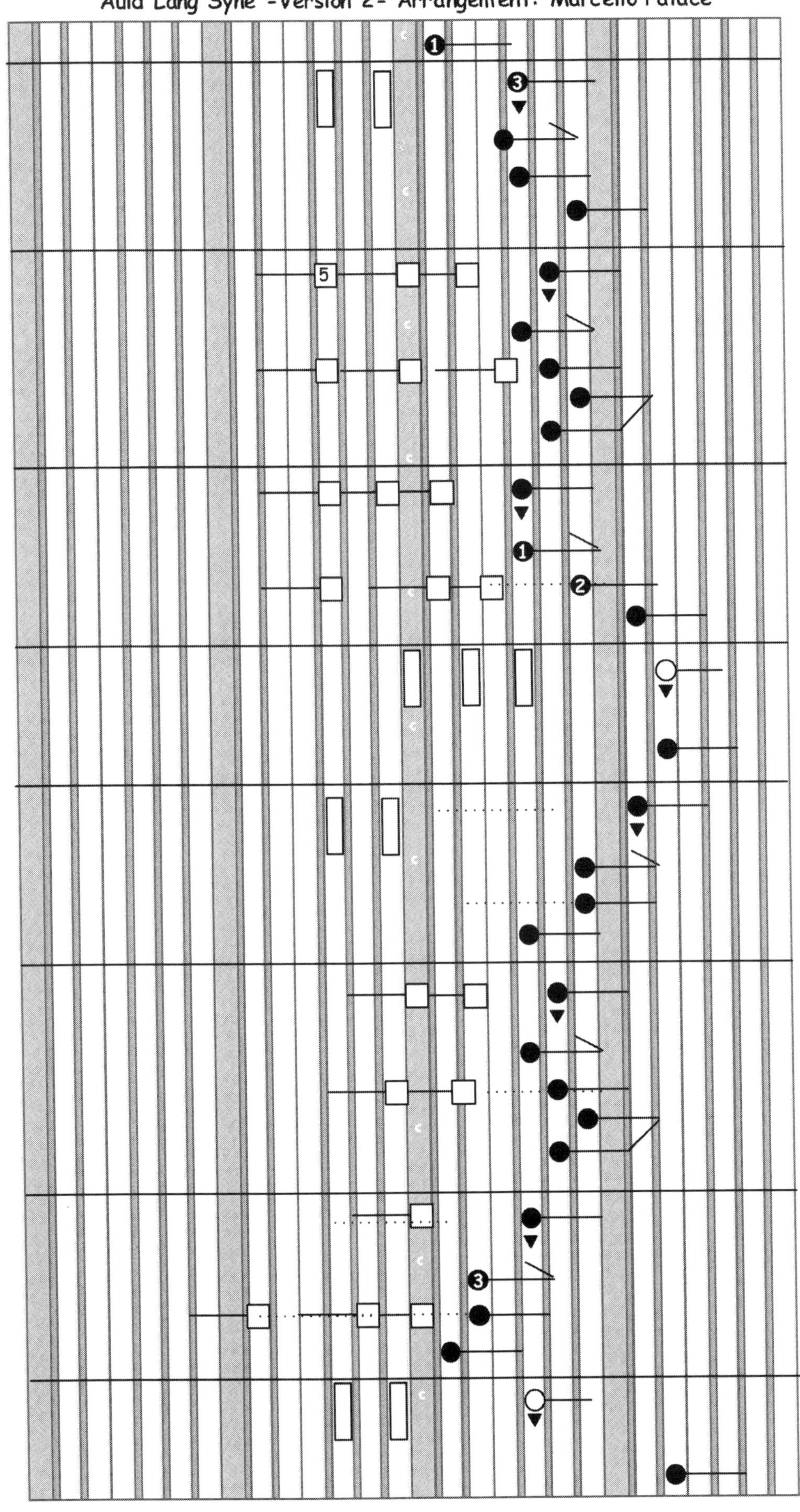

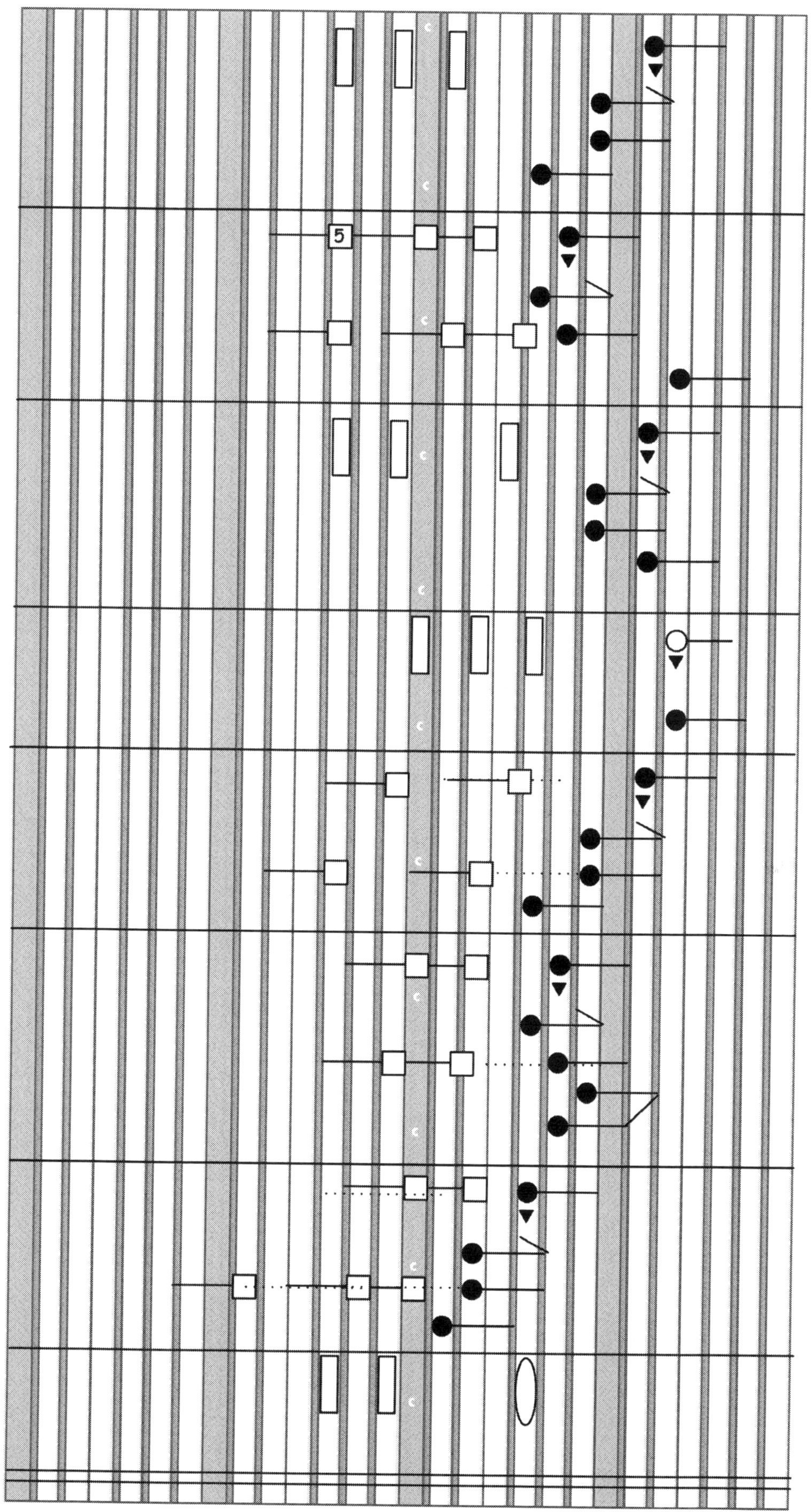
5

Scarborough Fair - Arranged by Marcello Palace

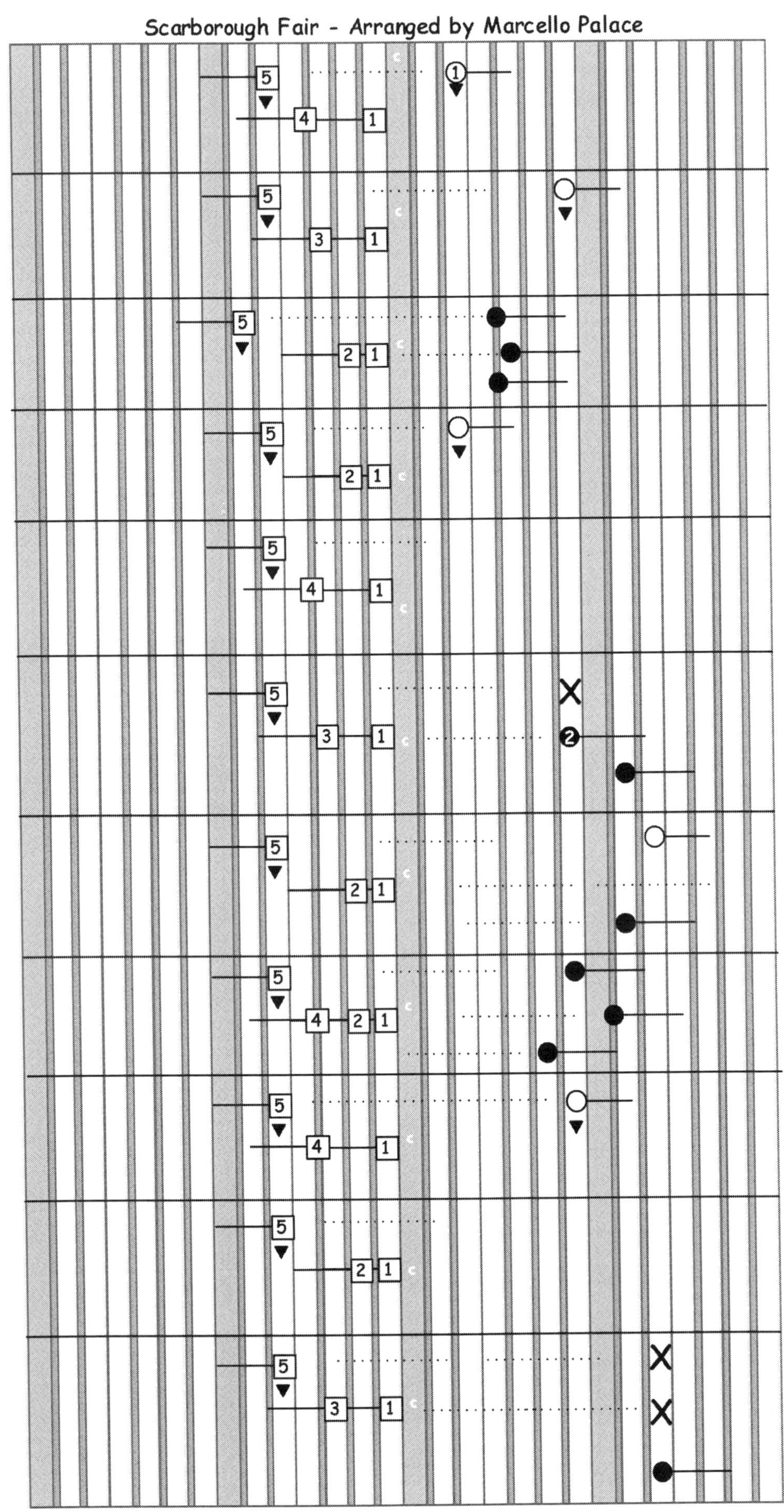

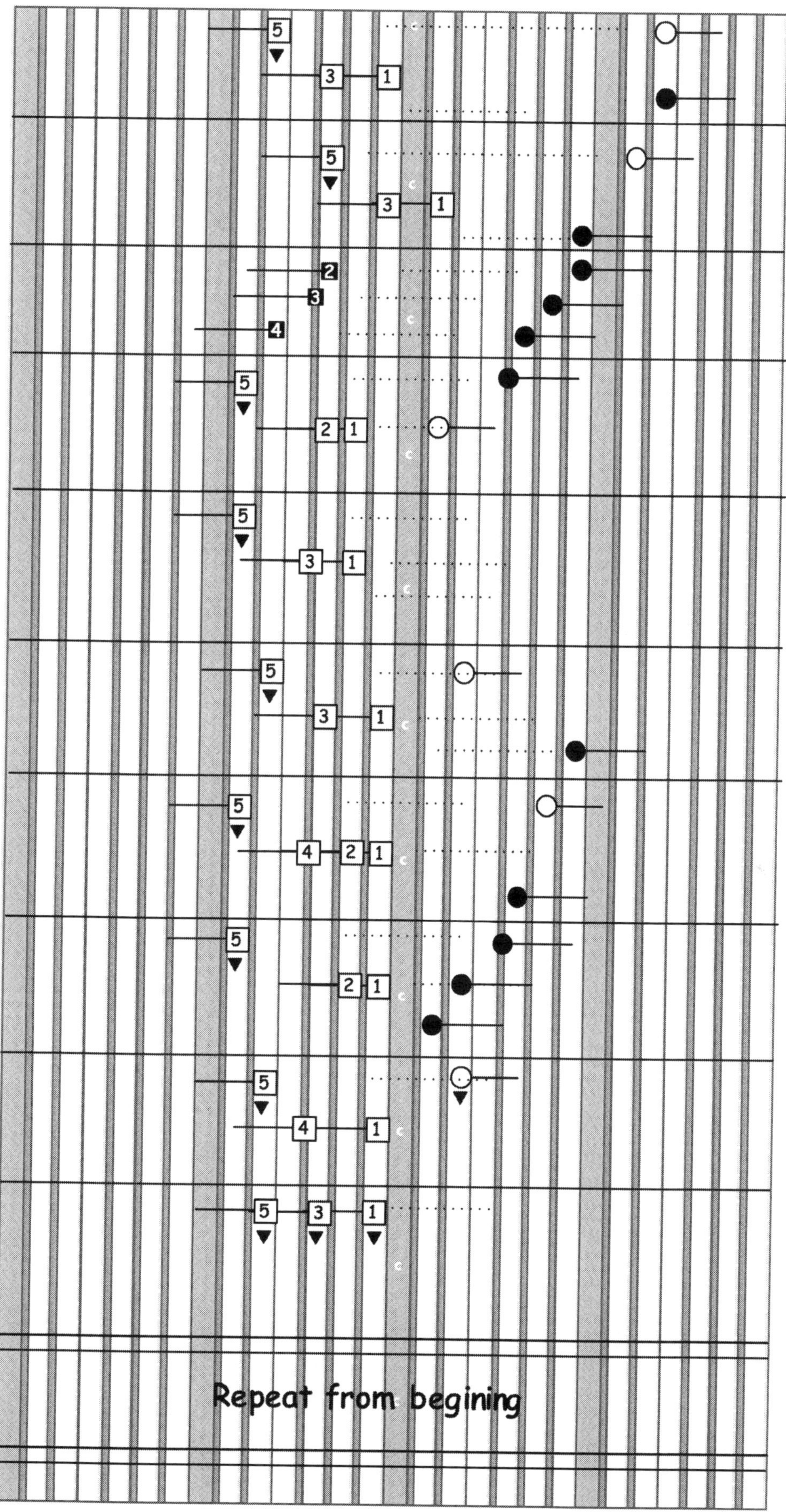
Repeat from begining

Gymnopedie no 1 - Eric Satie - Arranged by Marcello Palace

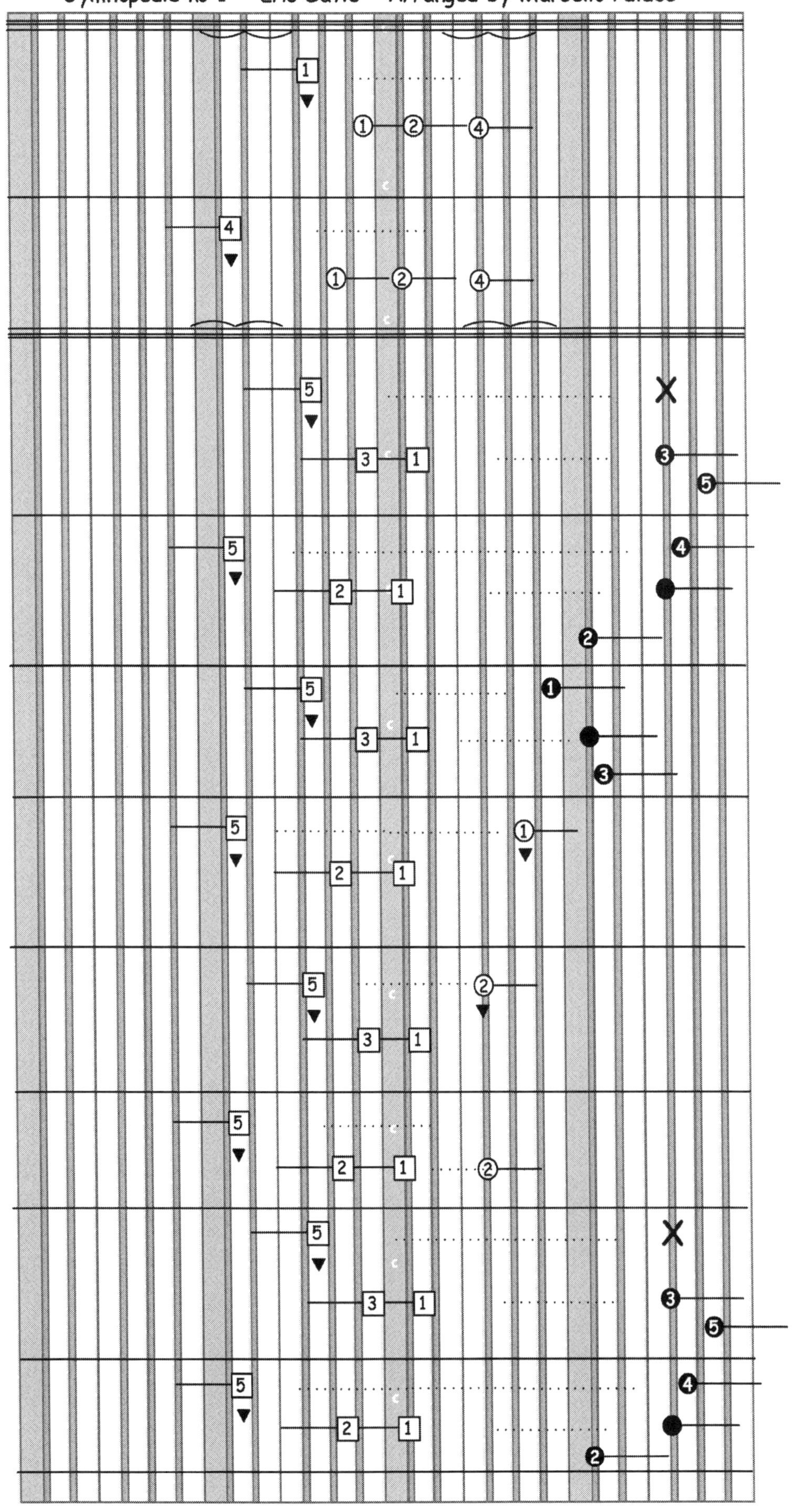

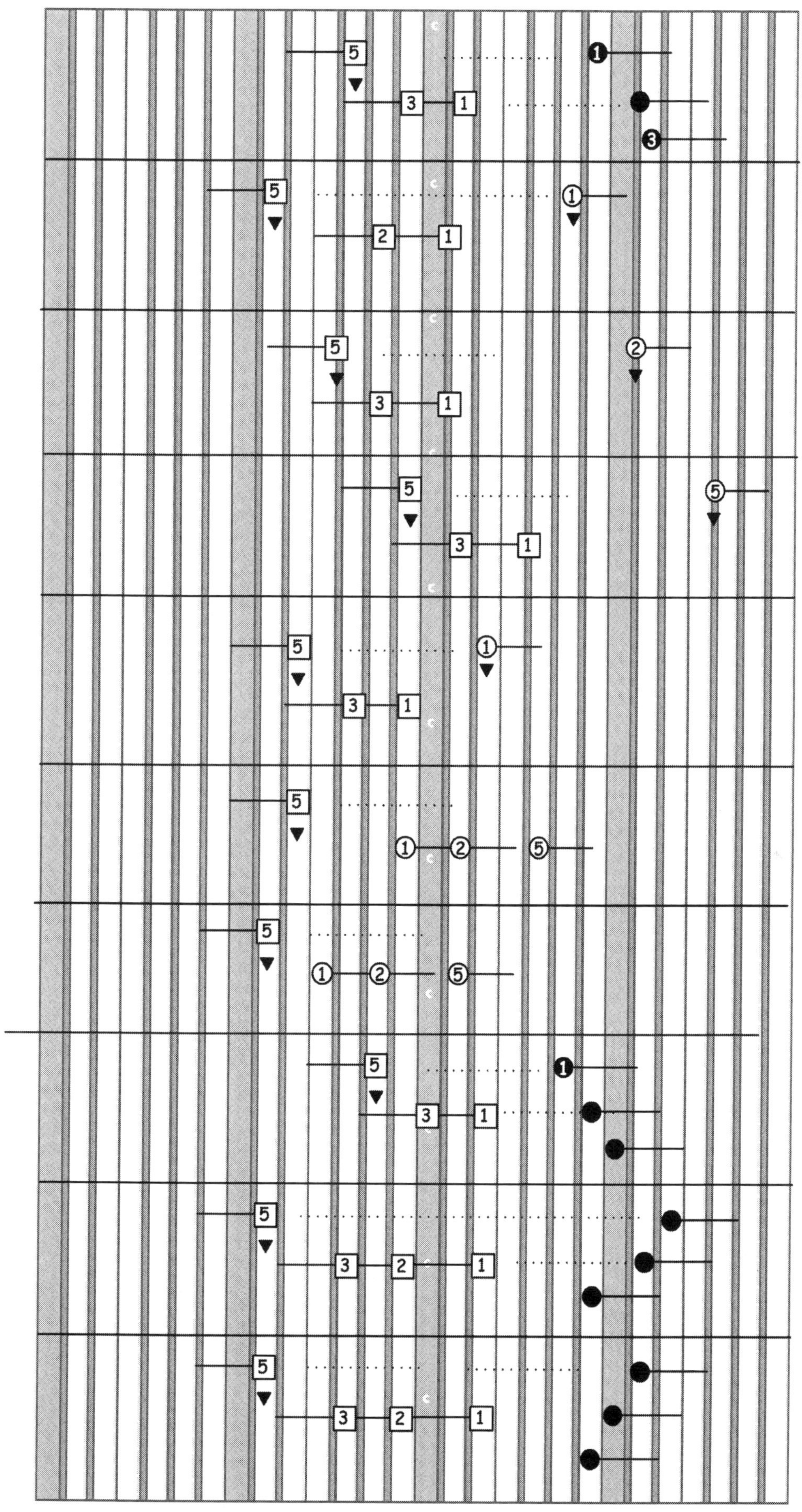

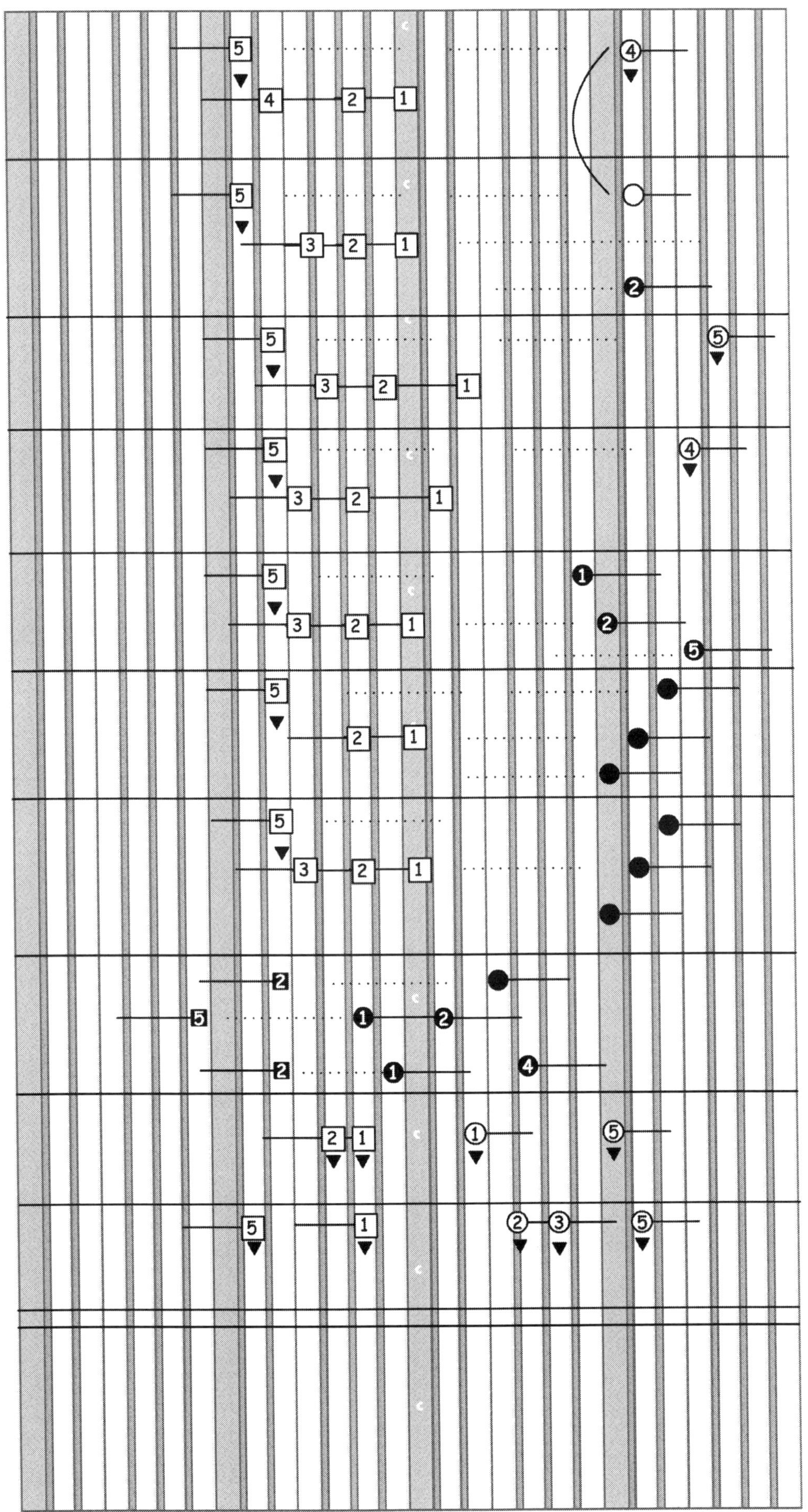

HOW TO PLAY THE MOONLIGHT SONATA

In this well know fragment of the first movement of Beethoven's Moonlight Sonata. We take as the unit the Quarter note. Setting every Quarter note to fit in a beat, the ideal tempo for this tune would be around the metronome speed of 100.

Although the Whole and the Half notes on the left hand would indicate the duration of four and two beats, let's be more flexible this time and take the right hand as a reference as for how long we keep the left hand ringing. In other words, keep the left hand pressing until the arrival of the next note, and a regular pulse on the right hand.

HOW TO PLAY THE ENTERTAINER

We included two versions of Scott Joplin's Entertainer. The difference between the two is that on the first version the left hand moves slower, in Whole notes steps, whilst on the second at twice the speed, in Half note steps.

In both cases we take as a unit the Quarter notes, so we play a Quarter per beat. A reasonable speed is to get to 200 but you can even go faster if you dear.

When we see the indication "*8va*" followed by an arrow pointing right, we play the enclosed fragment one octave up (seven white keys on the right). Watch out for the ties, for which we need to keep the right hand note pressed as we carry on playing notes on the left hand.

When Quarter notes are not ringing count four for a Whole note and two for a Half note in order to work out the exact duration of these notes. You will find pairs of "X" at certain points. As we explained before, these are rests, the right hand doesn't play but you still need to keep the count of a beat per cross.

HOW TO PLAY CLAIR DE LUNE

In this fragment of Debussy's *Clair de Lune*, we reach the maximum level of rhythmical freedom, in which the figures are just estimative and a reference to how long a note can last. This means that if we follow strictly the duration of the notes after setting a regular pulse for the piece, it will still sound recognisable but not quite musical.
The reason for this is to also open the Multiline system to those who prefer to follow the intuitive natural rhythm stored in their mind after getting familiar with the piece, rather than counting or working out the rhythm straight from the paper.

The best approach is therefore to listen to different versions of the piece -if you are not familiar with it- and then attempt to imitate what you heard, as you will now know what notes to play thanks to the Multiline part -and roughly for how long every note will lasts. Use a reasonable amount of sustain pedal if you can, in order to blend the sounds and to make it sound more impressionistic. Lift the pedal every time you cross a bar.

Moonlight - Beethoven (Fragment) - Arranged by Marcello Palace

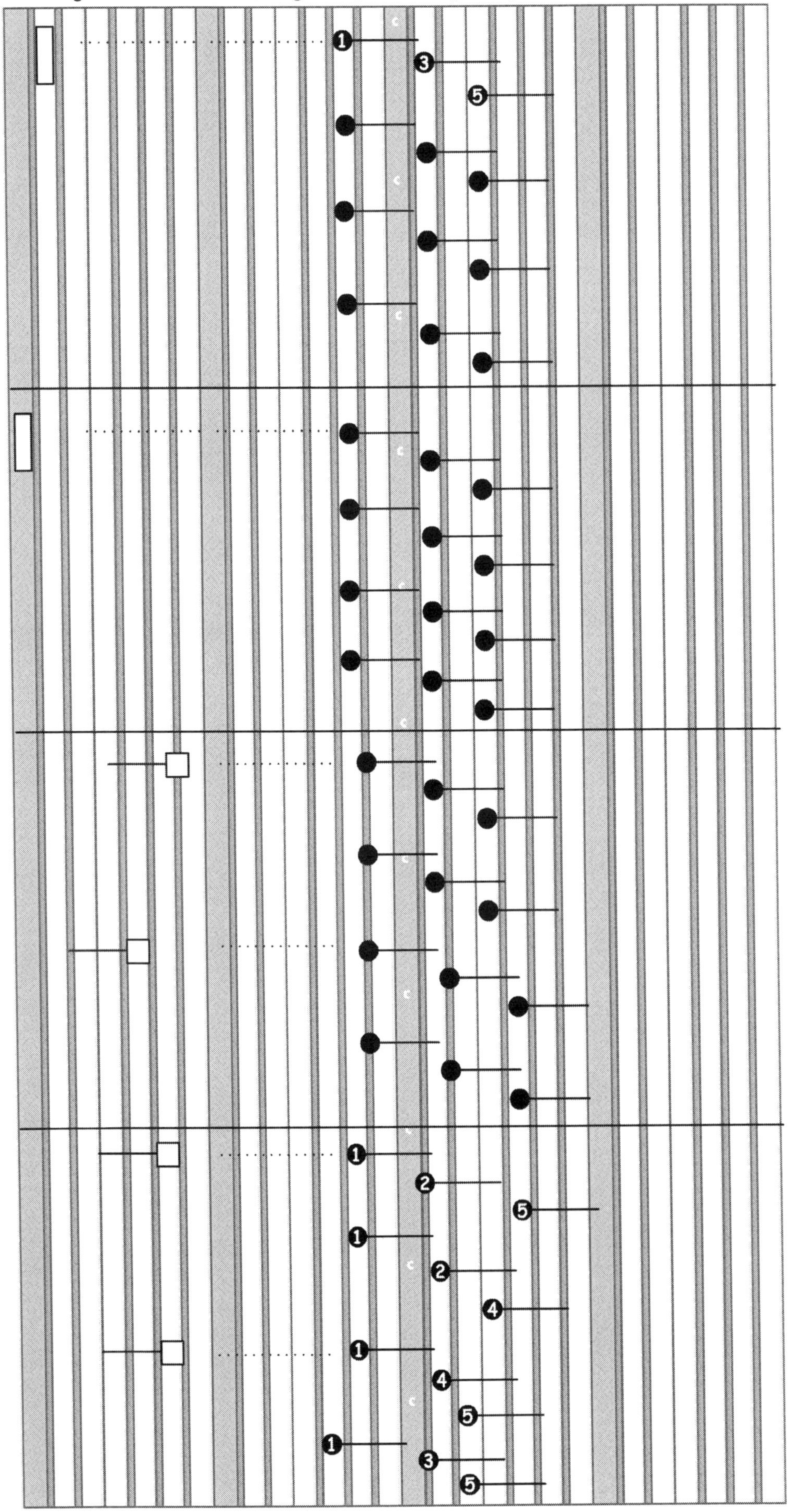

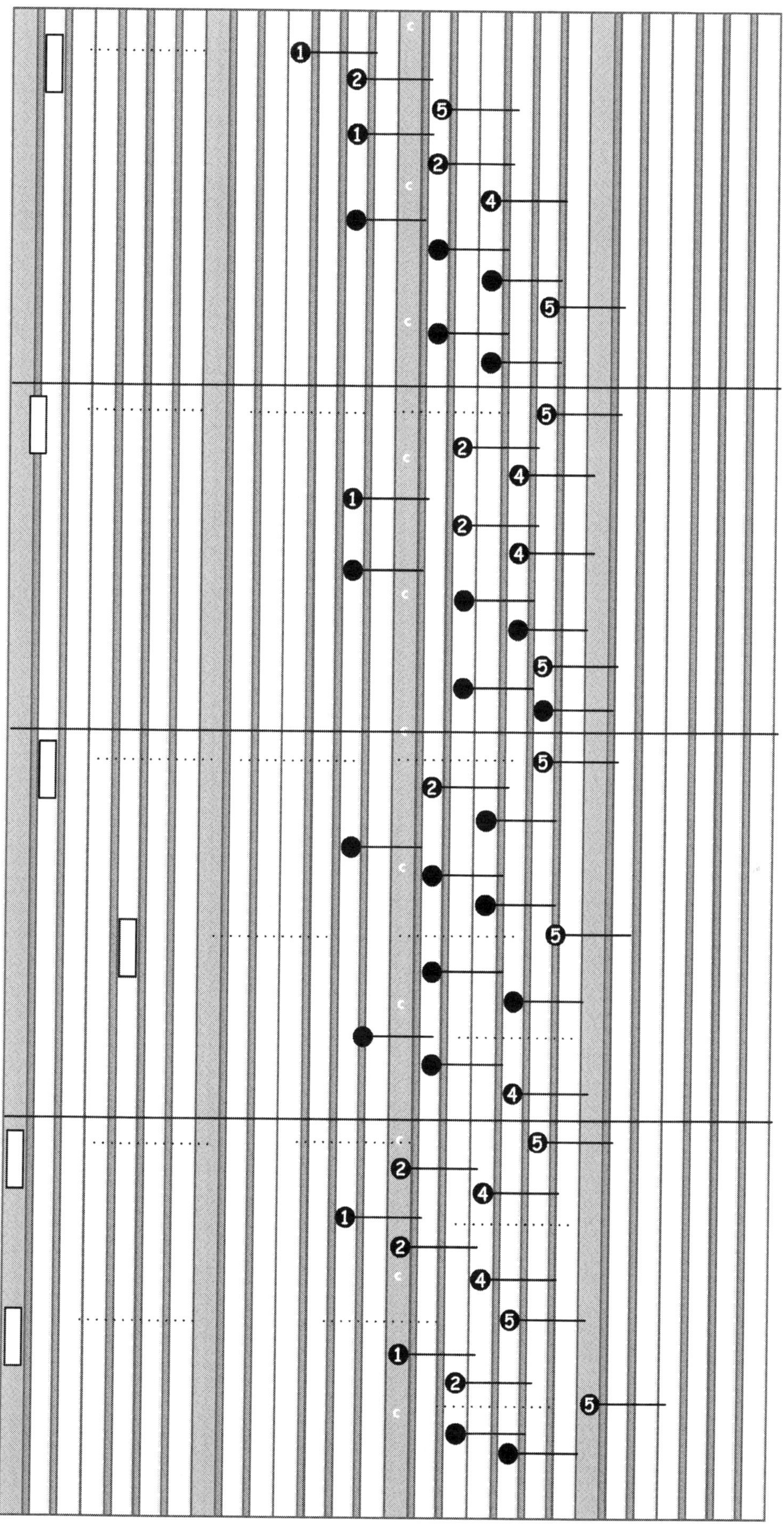

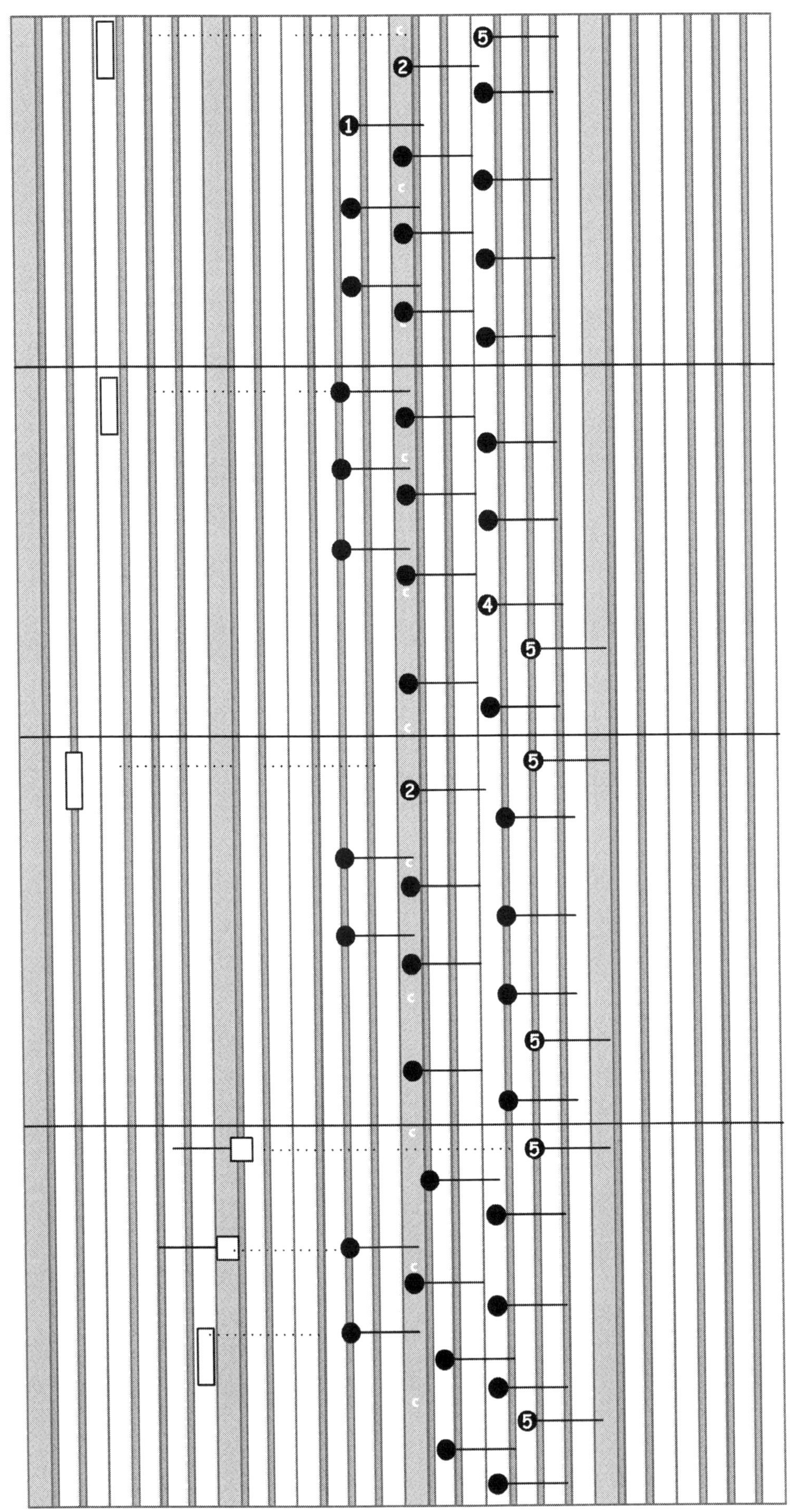

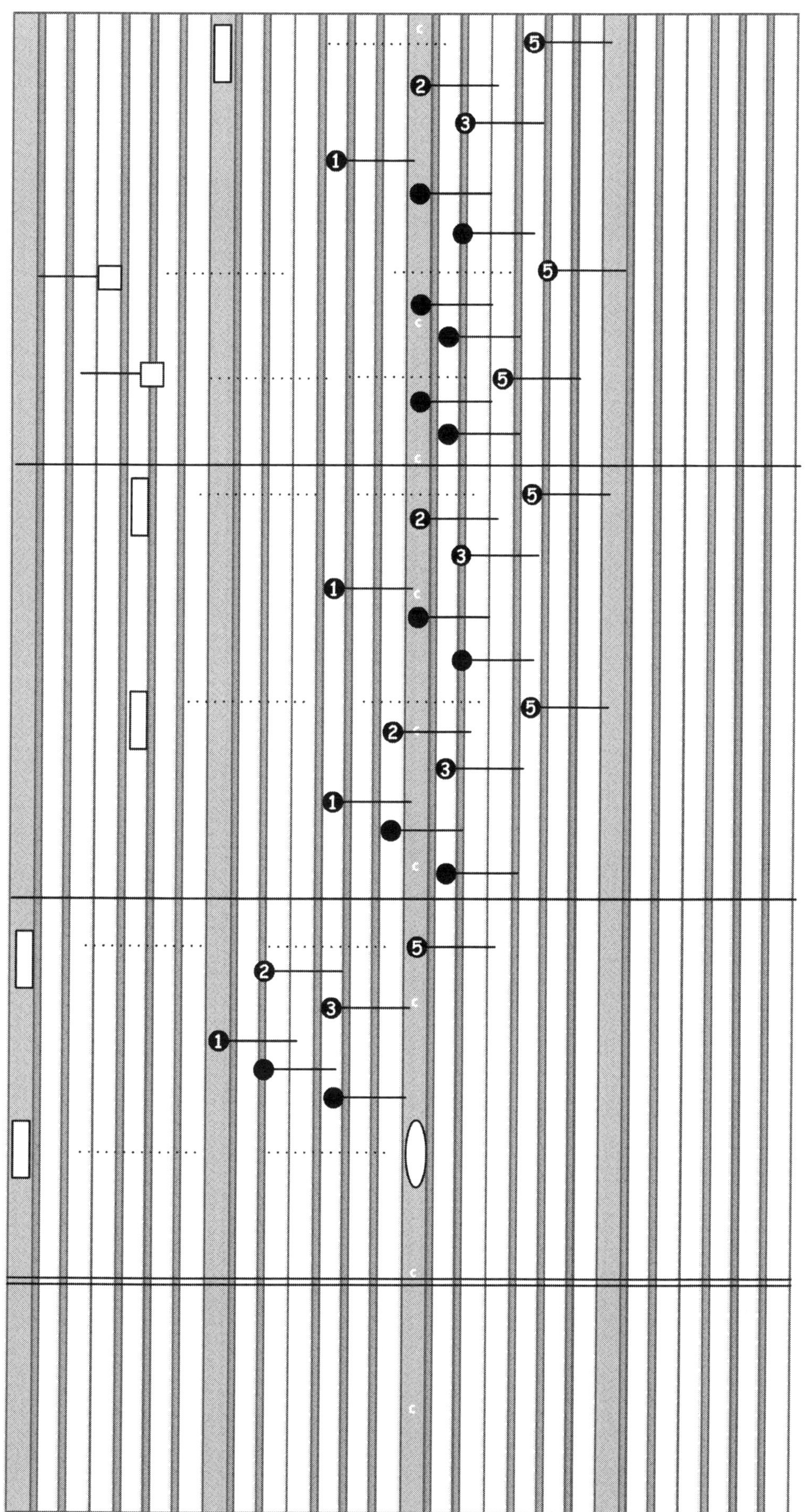

The Enterteiner - Joplin - Version 1 - Arranged by Marcello Palace

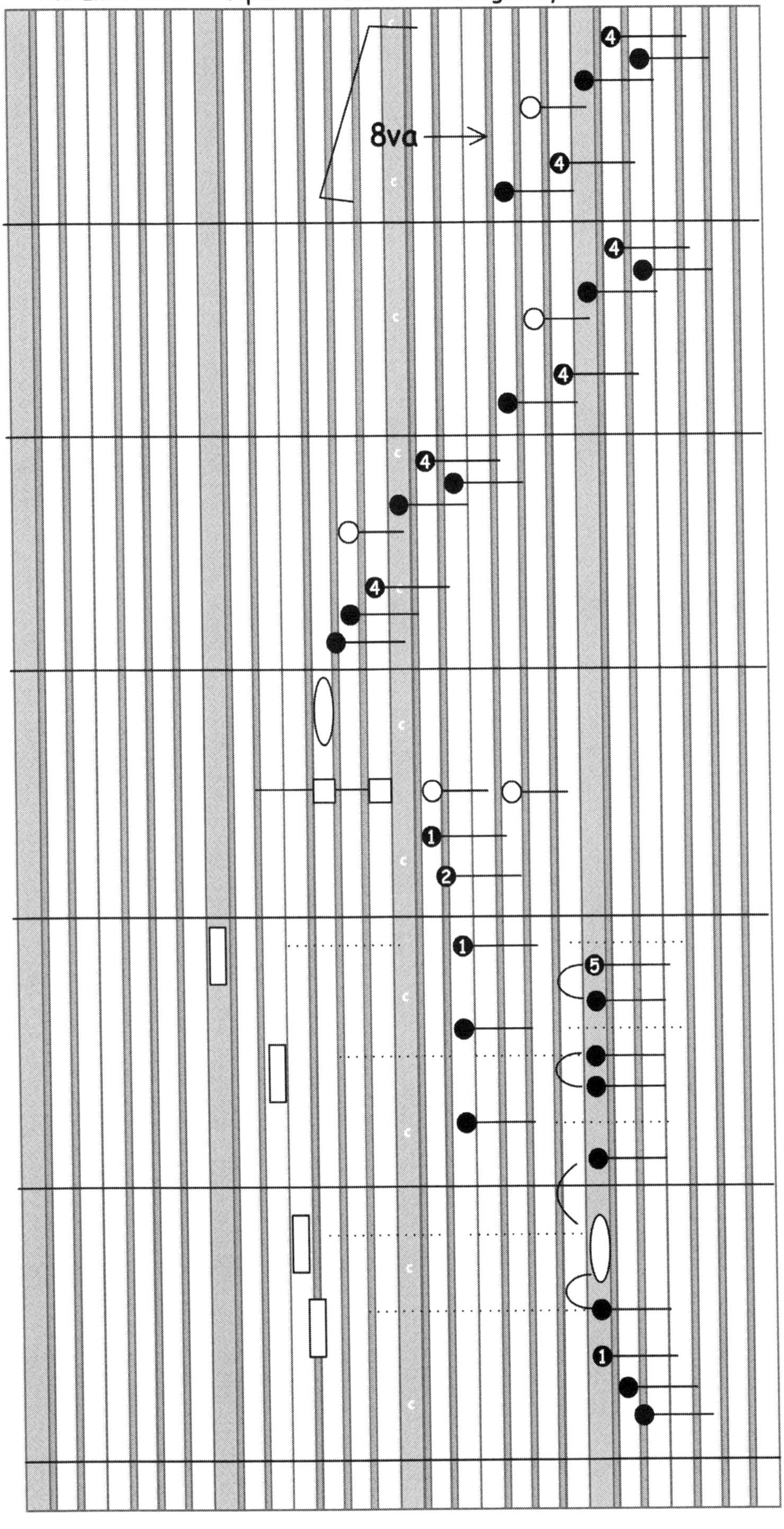

8va

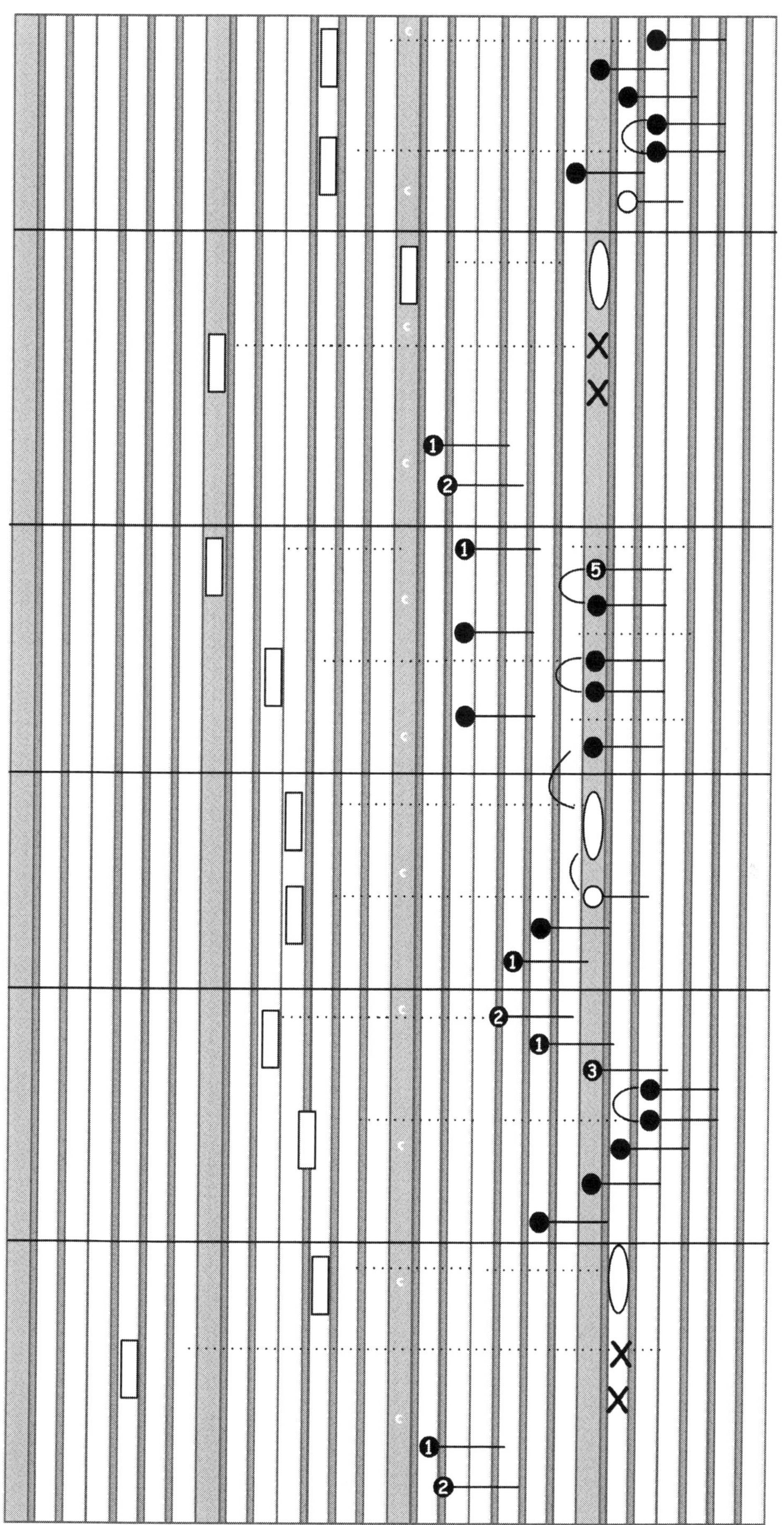

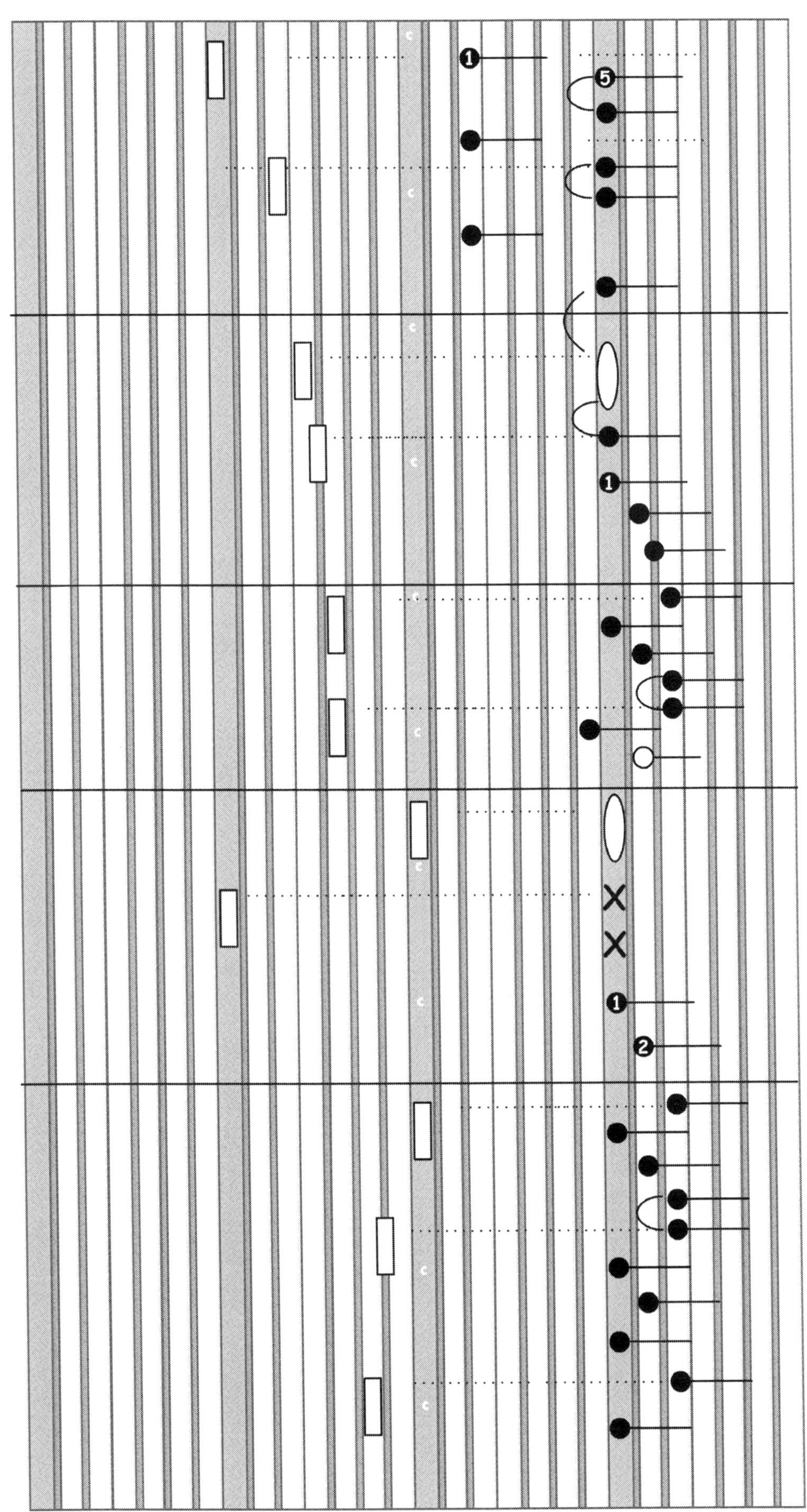

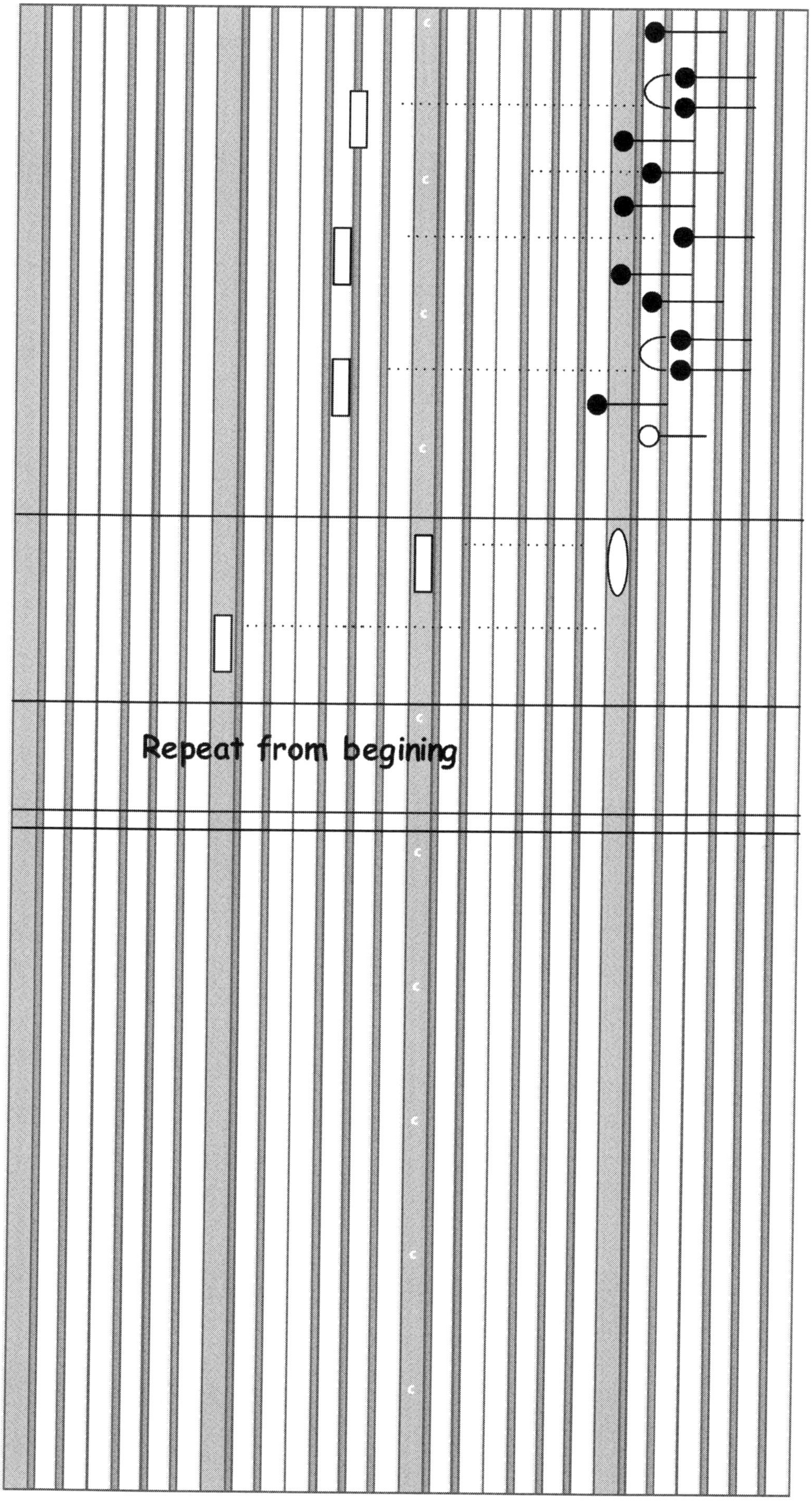

Repeat from begining

The Enterteiner - Joplin - Version 2 - Arranged by Marcello Palace

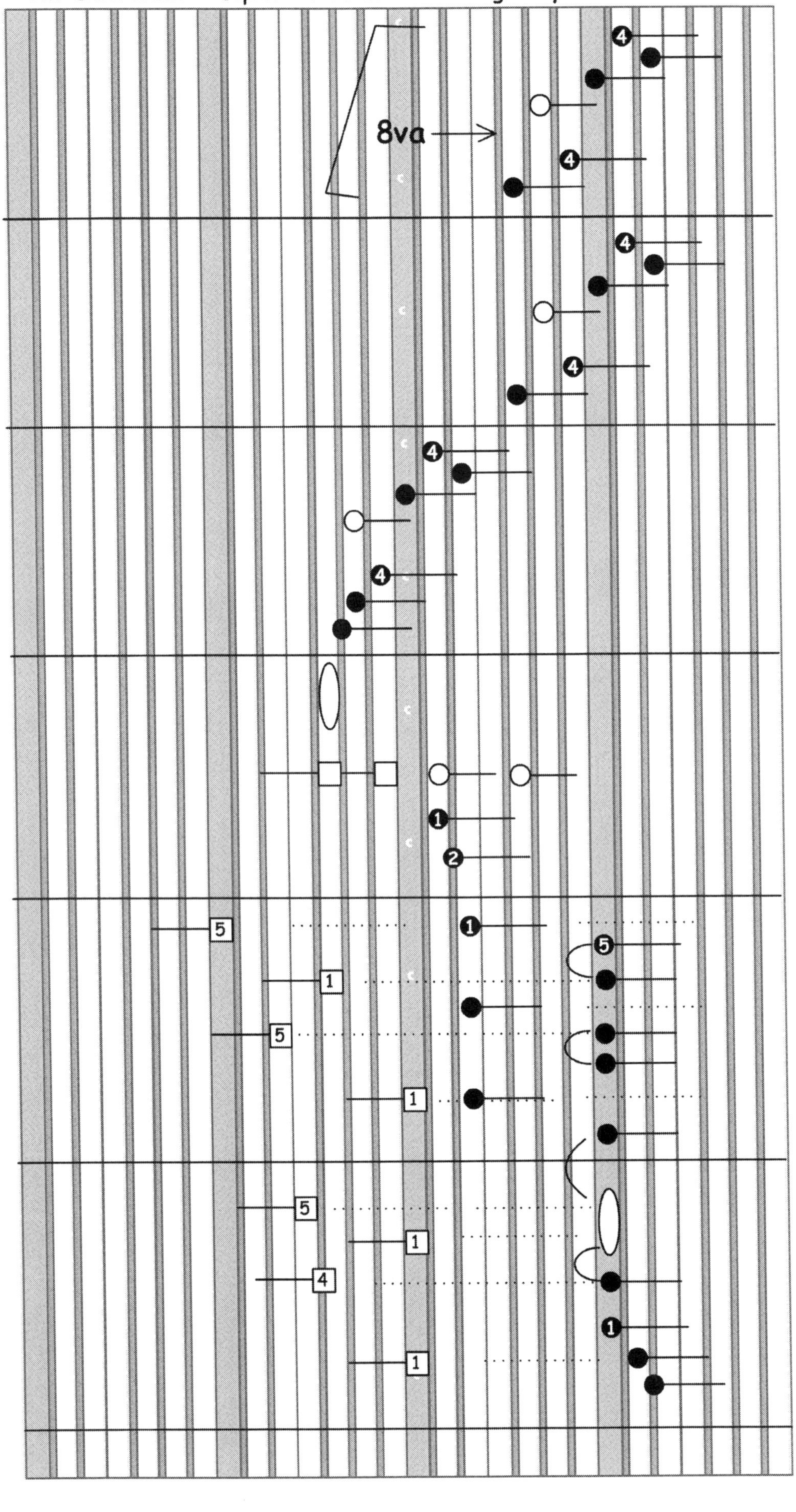

8va

4
4
4
4
4
4
1
2
5
1
5
5
1
5
1
4
1
1

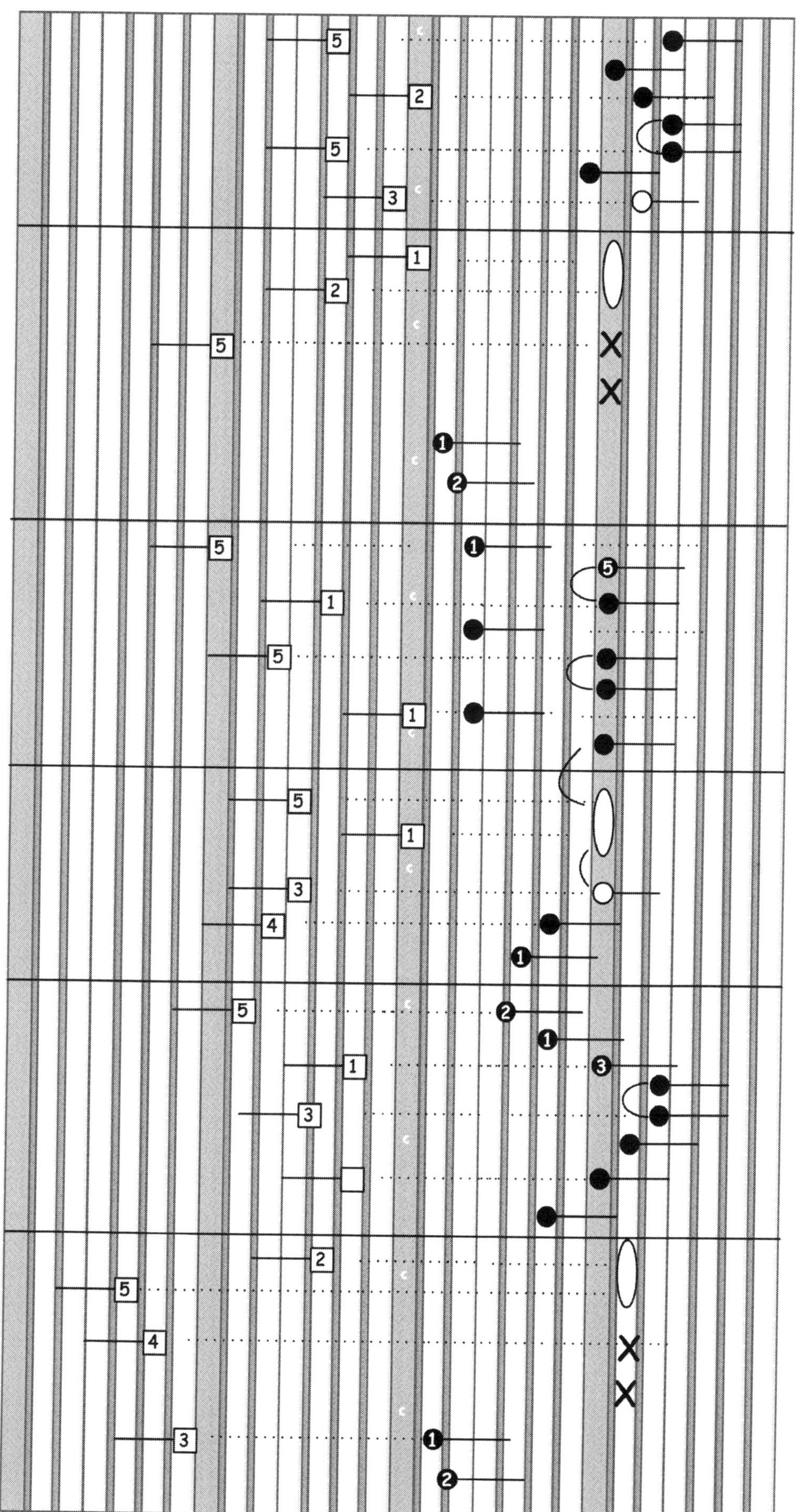

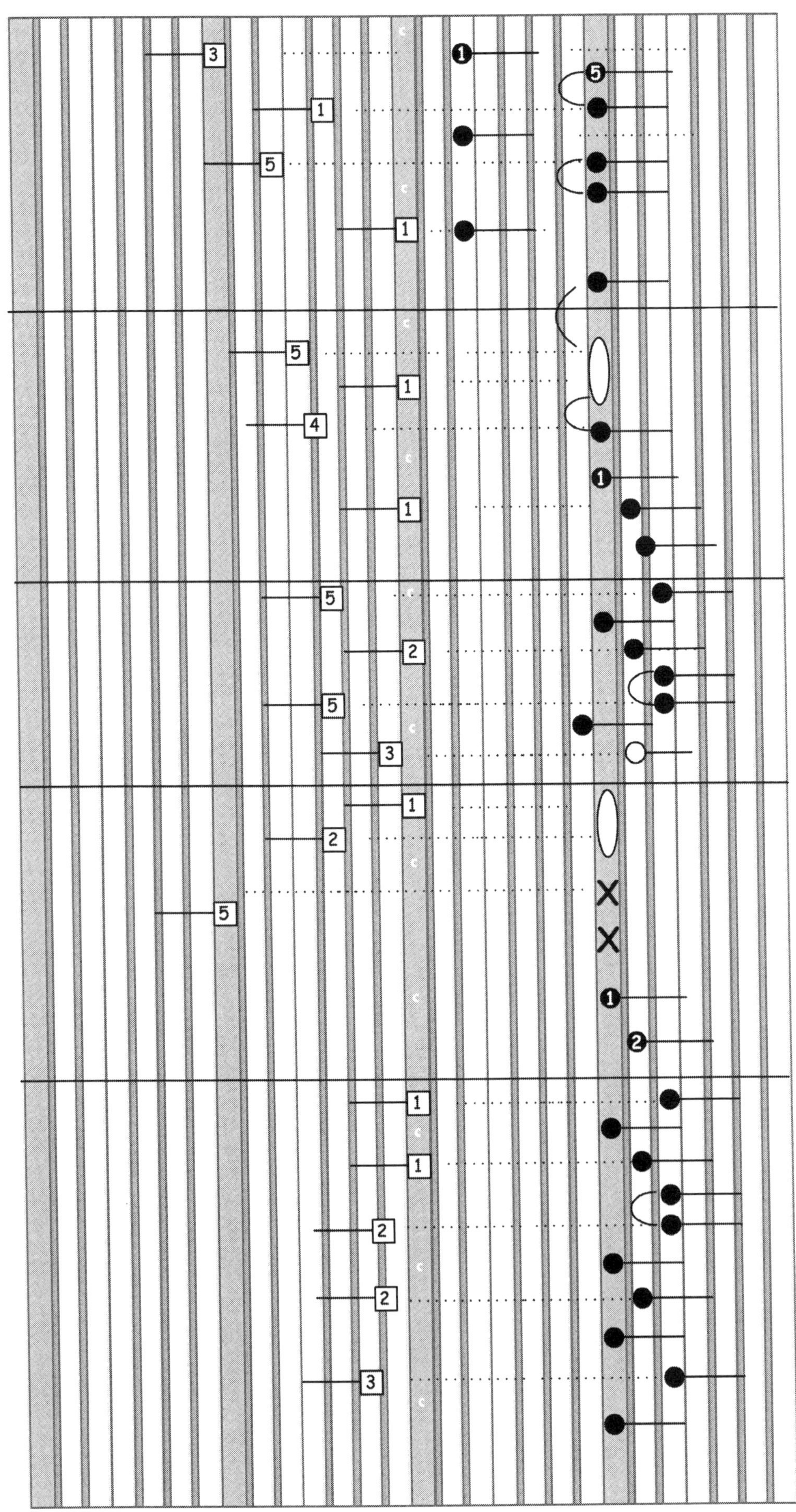

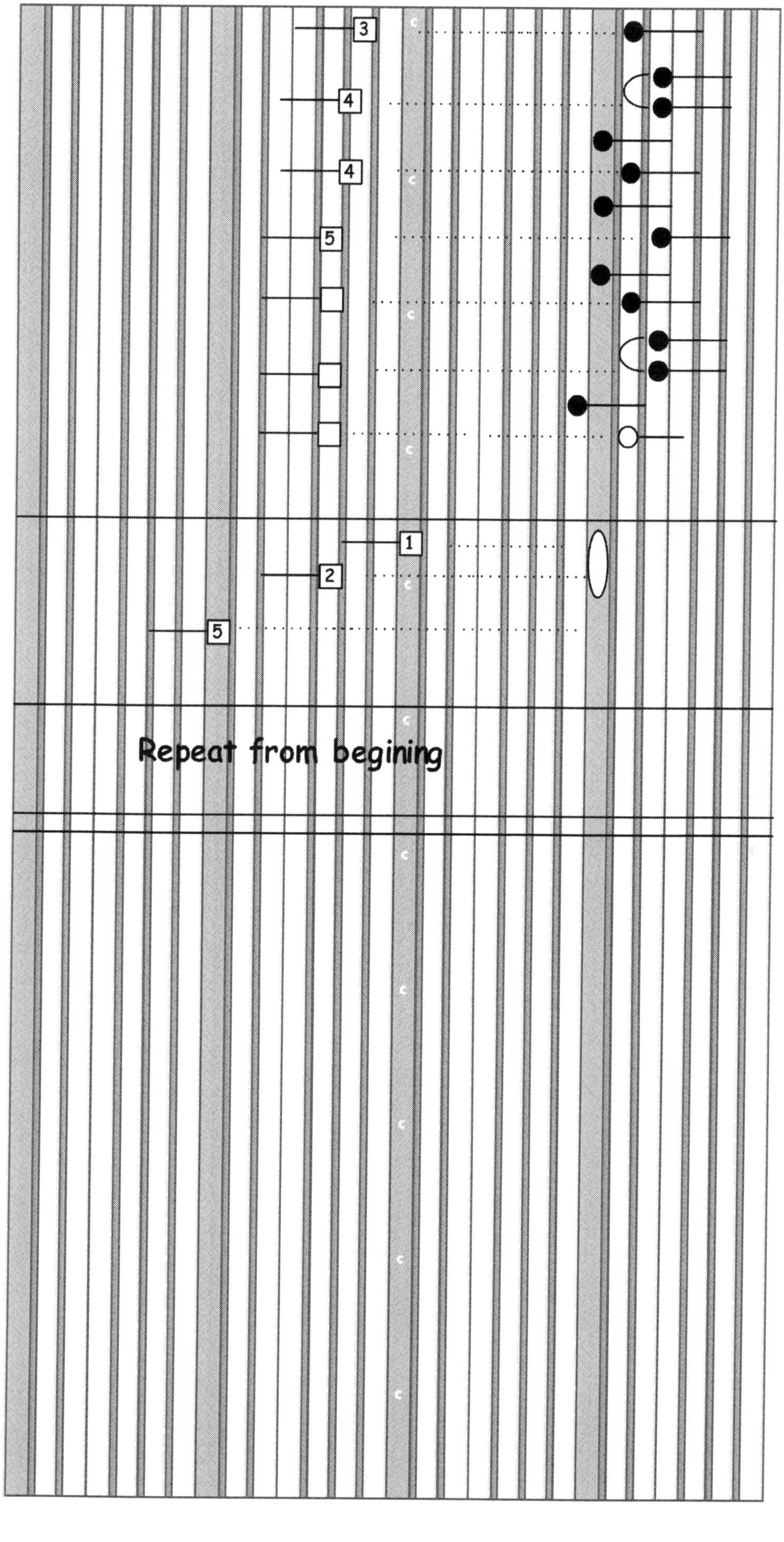

3

4

4

5

1

2

5

Repeat from begining

Clair de Lune - Claude Debussy - Arranged by Marcello Palace

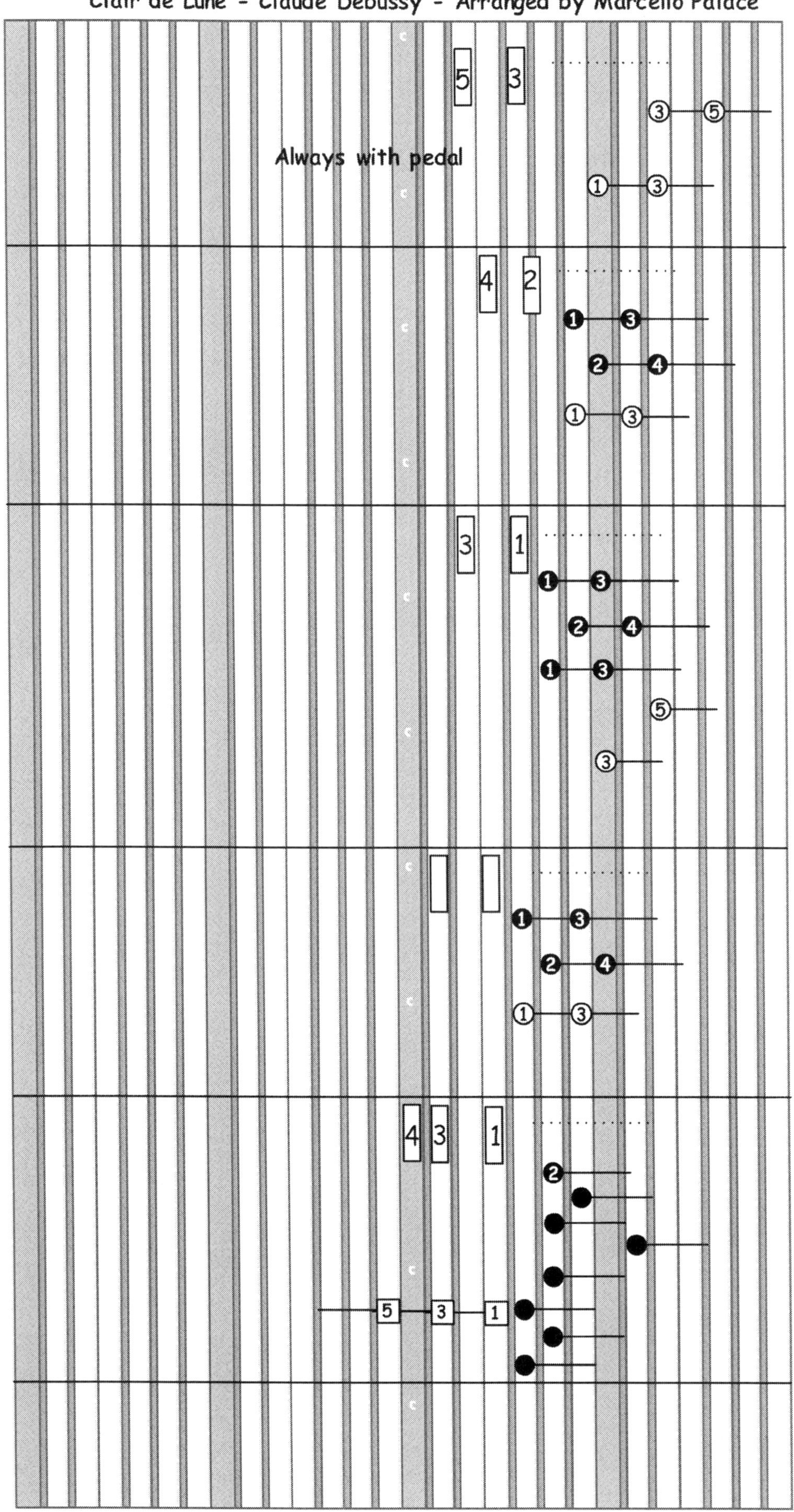

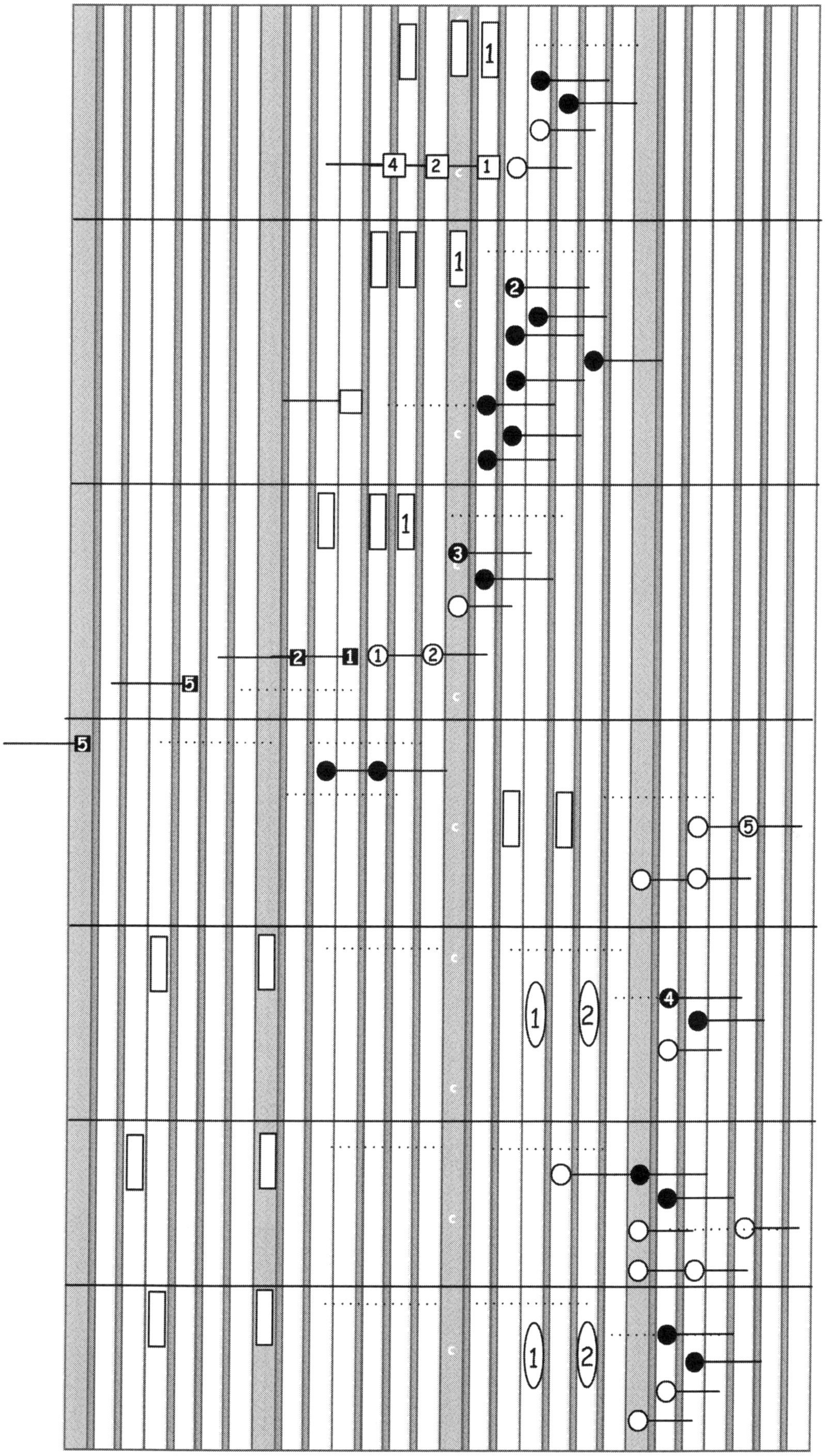

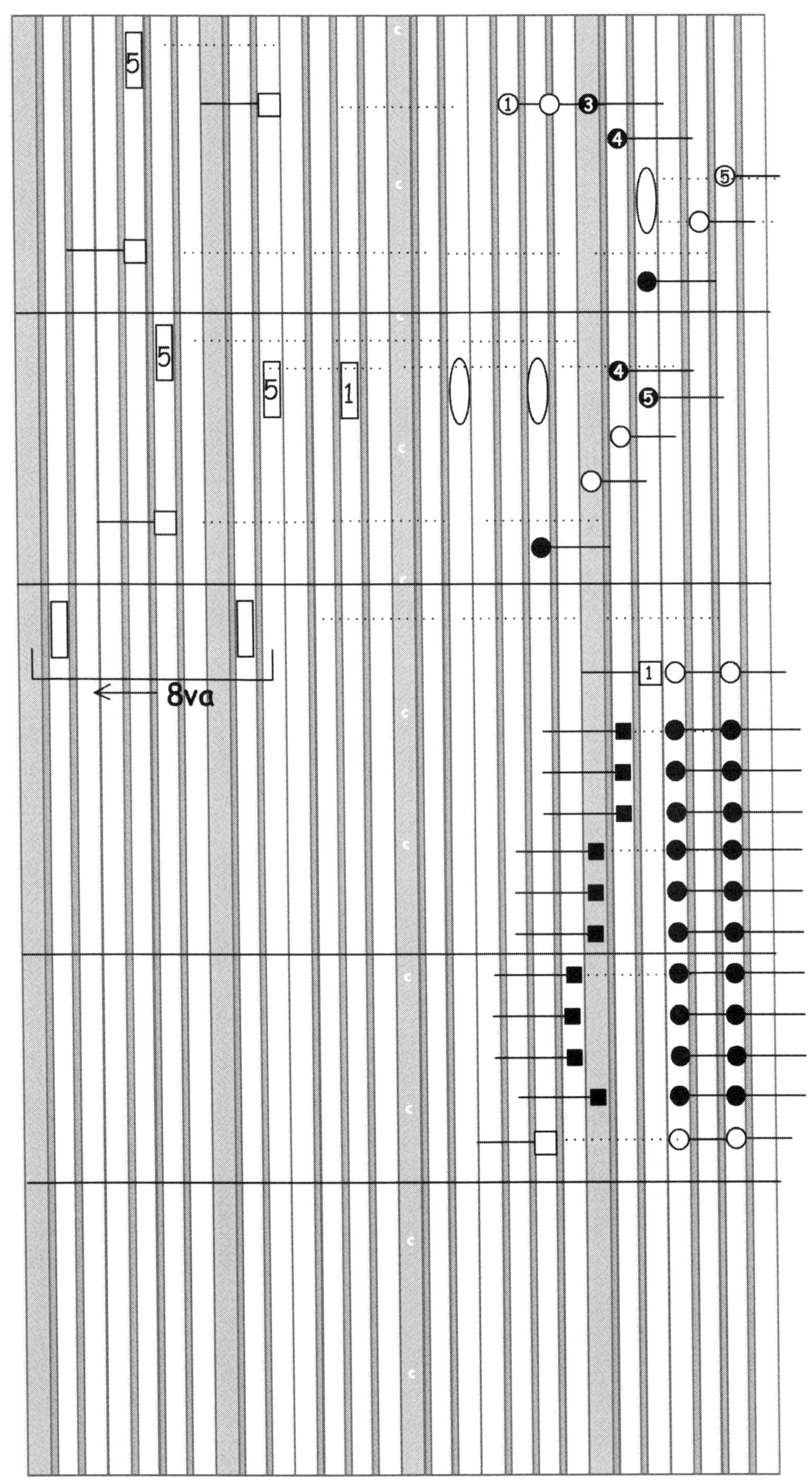

5
1
3
4
5
5
5
1
4
5
8va
1

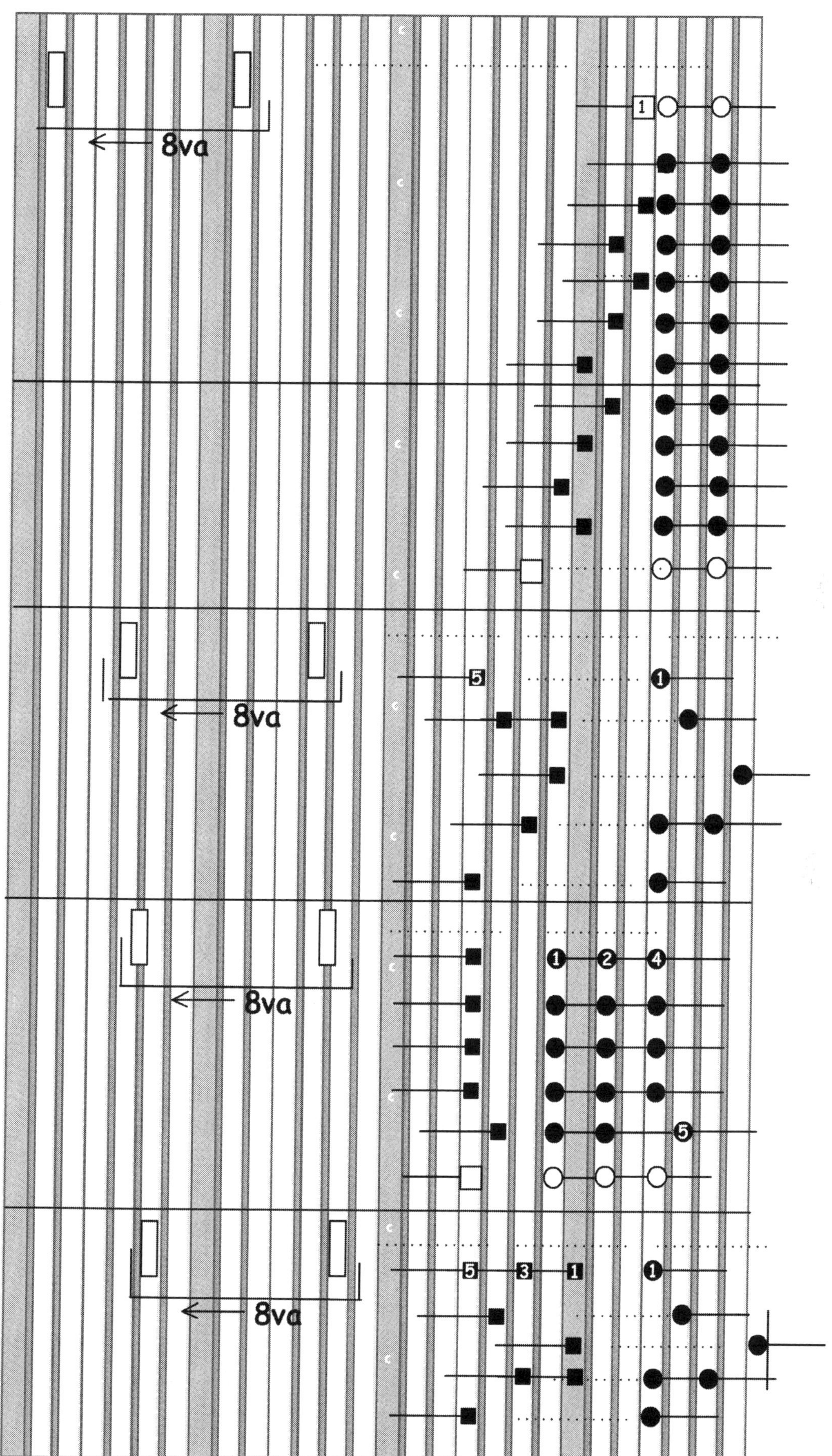

8va
1
8va
5
1
8va
1
2
4
5
8va
5
3
1
1

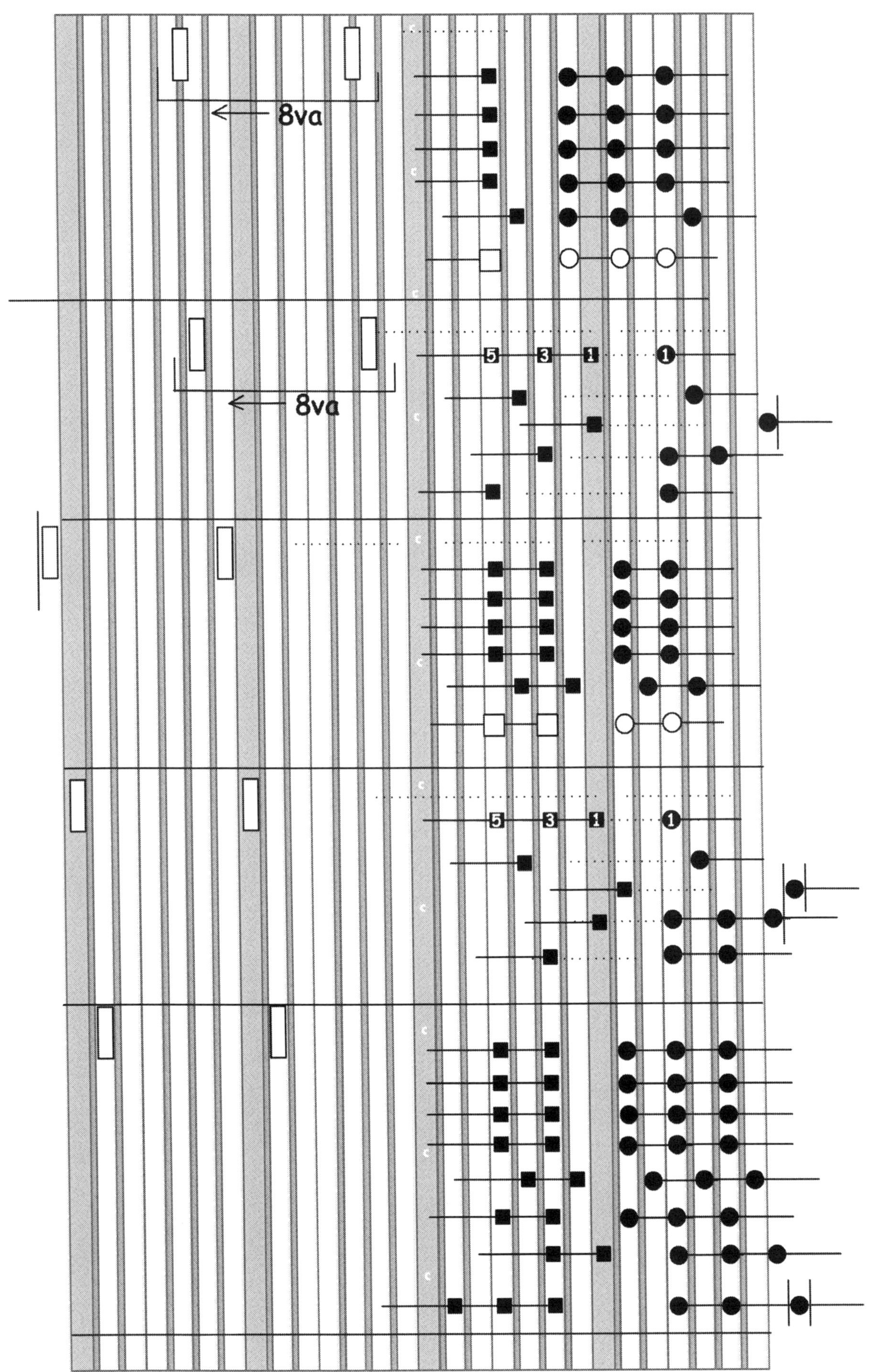
8va
8va
5
3
1
1
5
3
1
1

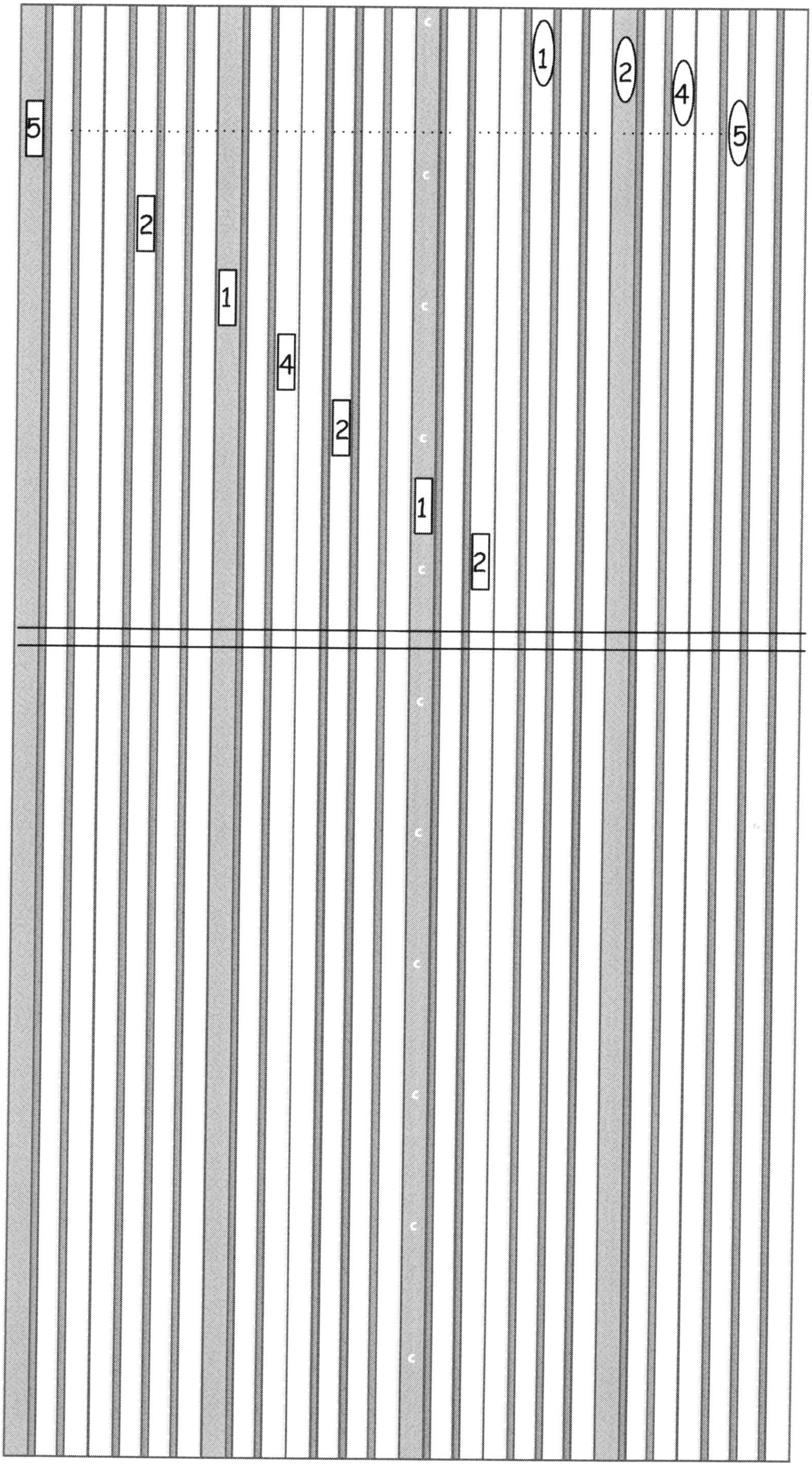
5
2
1
4
2
1
2
1
2
4
5

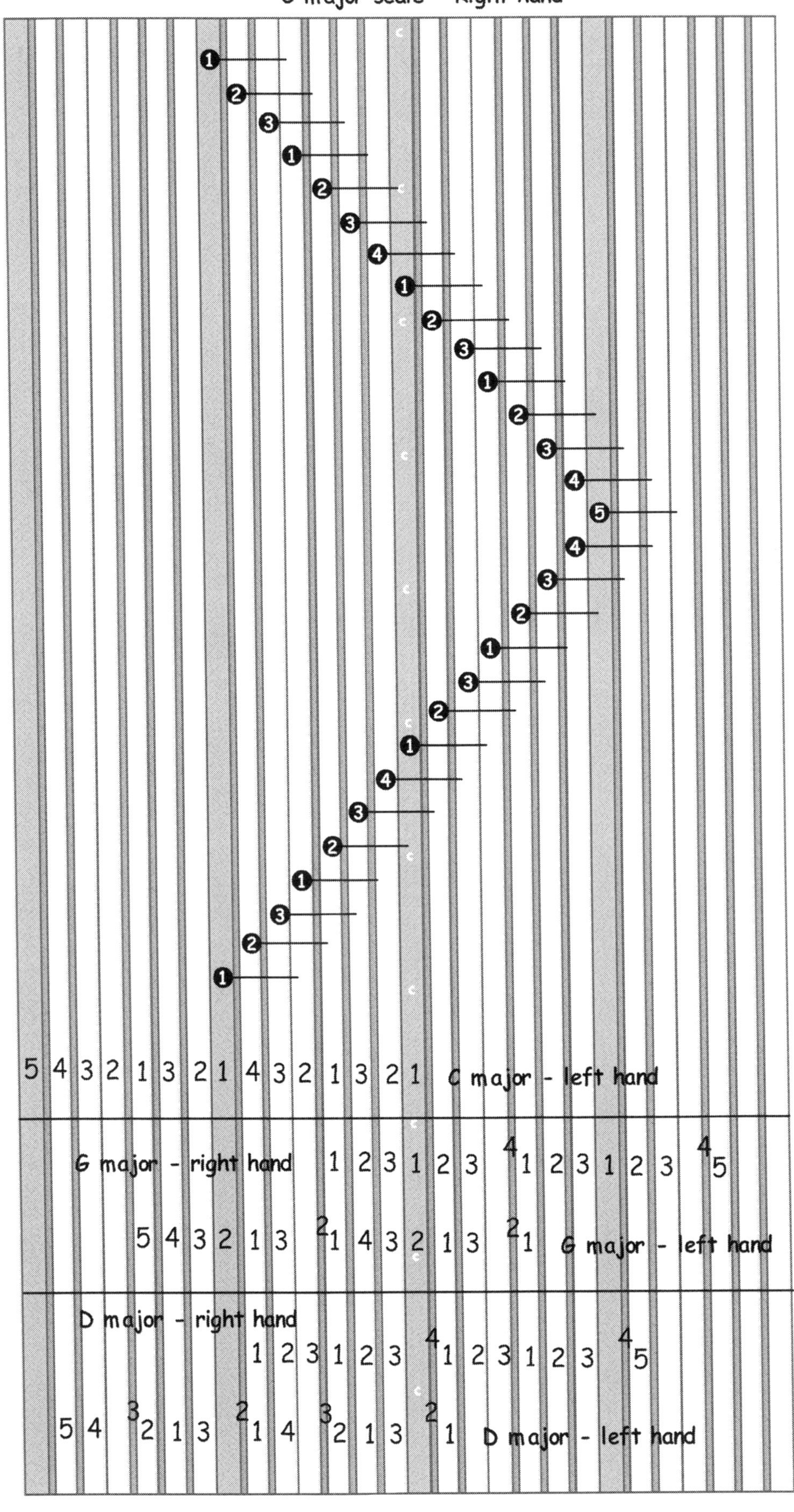
C major scale - Right hand
5 4 3 2 1 3 2 1 4 3 2 1 3 2 1 C major - left hand
G major - right hand 1 2 3 1 2 3 4 1 2 3 1 2 3 4 5
5 4 3 2 1 3 2 1 4 3 2 1 3 2 1 G major - left hand
D major - right hand
1 2 3 1 2 3 4 1 2 3 1 2 3 4 5
5 4 3 2 1 3 2 1 4 3 2 1 3 2 1 D major - left hand

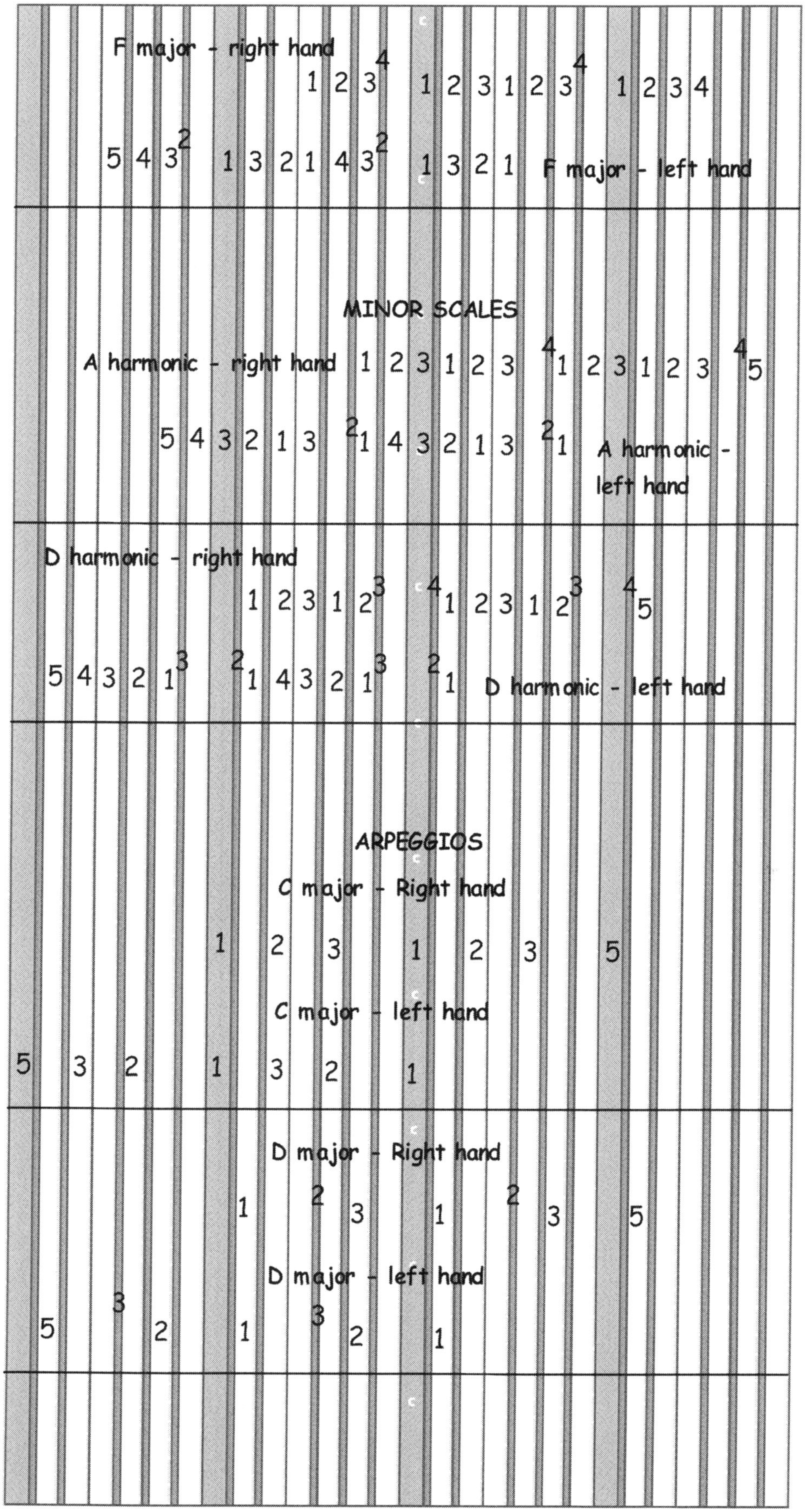

F major - right hand

1 2 3 4 1 2 3 1 2 3 4 1 2 3 4

5 4 3 2 1 3 2 1 4 3 2 1 3 2 1 F major - left hand

MINOR SCALES

A harmonic - right hand 1 2 3 1 2 3 4 1 2 3 1 2 3 4 5

5 4 3 2 1 3 2 1 4 3 2 1 3 2 1 A harmonic - left hand

D harmonic - right hand

1 2 3 1 2 3 4 1 2 3 1 2 3 4 5

5 4 3 2 1 3 2 1 4 3 2 1 3 2 1 D harmonic - left hand

ARPEGGIOS

C major - Right hand

1 2 3 1 2 3 5

C major - left hand

5 3 2 1 3 2 1

D major - Right hand

1 2 3 1 2 3 5

D major - left hand

5 3 2 1 3 2 1

LEARNING SOME SCALES AND ARPEGGIOS WITH MULTILINE

The KeyLang Multiline is a very handy tool to learn the scales and arpeggios. We include in these last pages a sample of a typical C scale for the right hand with the most commonly accepted fingering.

In order to simplify the representation of an scale, we present the rest of the scales with this format, in this case the left hand C major scale:

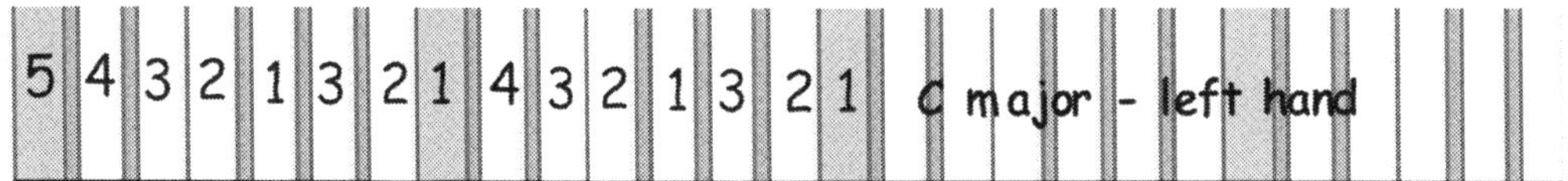

Observing the fingering, move from the left to the right and back to the left.

We're also learning to play arpeggios, like this one:

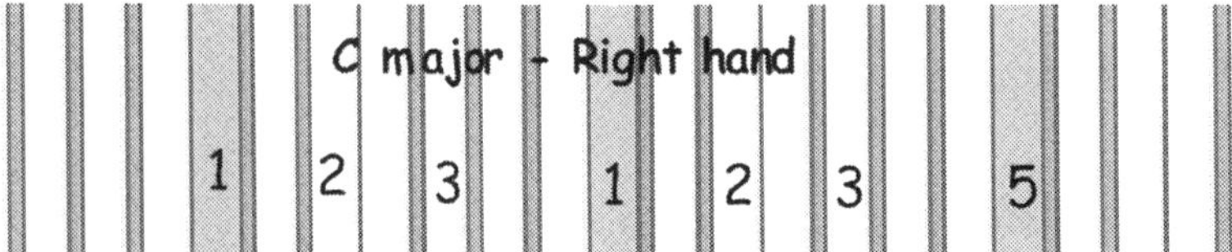

Once again, observing the fingering we move from the left to the right of the keyboard and then came back to the left. Arpeggios are like scales that skip one or two notes.

Scales and arpeggios are good tool to develop keyboard skill. They allow us to play a succession of notes without interruptions in between, when we are playing actual pieces.

LICENCE FOR THE USE OF THE KEYLANG MULTILINE [MT] SYSTEM TO PUBLISH YOUR OWN CREATIONS AND ARRANGEMENTS

There are certain restrictions to publish music written in KeyLang Multiline [MT] system:

1- Web-page postings, **without any commercial purposes**, of your own arrangements and compositions are allowed only if quoting "in KeyLang Multiline " somewhere on the page.
2- **Publication made with commercial purposes are strictly forbidden**. It is not allowed to charge a fee to access any online page containing music written in Multiline System.
3- The author and the publishers are not held responsible for any external source publication written in Multiline that violates the law of the Copyright.
4- Lessons or Training session using the Multiline System with commercial purpose is strictly forbidden.
5- Publications on paper of music written in Multiline are strictly forbidden without prior written authorisation of the creators of KeyLang Multiline [MT].

BLANK SHEET

We include a blank sheet of Multiline paper so you can also write your own music and arrangements.

Contents

14238217R00040

Made in the USA
Lexington, KY
16 March 2012